Dear Ronnie

A Friendship in Letters

Also by Michael Shaw

The Fin-de-Siècle Scottish Revival:
Romance, Decadence and Celtic Identity

A Friendship in Letters

Robert Louis Stevenson
& J. M. Barrie

Edited by
MICHAEL SHAW

SANDSTONE PRESS

First published in Great Britain by
Sandstone Press Ltd
Willow House
Stoneyfield Business Park
Inverness
IV2 7PA
Scotland

www.sandstonepress.com

The editor would like to thank the Estate of
Robert Louis Stevenson for their support
with publishing Stevenson's letters.

ISBN: 978-1-913207-02-1
ISBNe: 978-1-913207-03-8

Designed by *Jules Akel*
Printed and bound by *CPI Group (UK) Ltd*, Croydon, CR0 4YY

for Tusitala and Softy Softy

Contents

Introduction

ON MONDAY 13 AUGUST 1894, RESIDENTS IN MUSKEGON, MICHIGAN OPENED THEIR local newspaper, the *Muskegon Chronicle*, to discover that two of the most popular and critically acclaimed writers of the day—Robert Louis Stevenson and J. M. Barrie—were engaged in correspondence. Adorned with illustrations of both writers, the paper's gossip column ran an article on their rumoured friendship, which noted that they had become the 'warmest friends', with Barrie known to write 'reams of letters to Stevenson'. The *Muskegon Chronicle* wasn't alone. From Dundee to Massachusetts, from Illinois to Alabama, newspapers were carrying the story that a friendship between Stevenson and Barrie had blossomed through correspondence.[1]

....

1. 'Barrie and Stevenson', *Muskegon Chronicle*, 13 August 1894, p. 4. The correspondence was reported in *The Dundee Courier*, *The Sunday Herald* (Boston), *Birmingham Age-Herald* (Alabama), and *The Morning Star* (Rockford, Illinois), among other newspapers.

Many famous writers wrote to each other on a regular basis in the late-Victorian era—correspondences that wouldn't necessarily be considered newsworthy. What drew the press to the Stevenson-Barrie correspondence was its peculiarity. Despite both attending Edinburgh University in the 1870s and having several friends in common, the two authors had never met in person and were now living at opposite ends of the earth: Stevenson had settled in Samoa by the time their friendship began in 1892, while Barrie was living between Kirriemuir in Angus and London. As a result, the letters took a distinctive form: in attempting to showcase their personality to one another, they were often revealing, open and gossipy, which the press had picked up on. '[They] know all each other's secrets and affairs, yet they have never seen one another', reported the *Muskegon Chronicle*. Stevenson's wife (Fanny Van de Grift) later expressed her view that the letter-based friendship gave the correspondence a particular charm. Commenting on Stevenson's body of letters after he died, she said: 'perhaps the gayest of them all are directed to Mr. Barrie, of whom Louis was very fond, although they had never met. Their friendship was carried on entirely by correspondence, and so Louis's letters were, in

a way, autobiographical'.[2] This autobiographical element (which was equally evident in Barrie's letters) excited prospective readers, and it was hoped that the correspondence would soon be published. The author of the article that appeared in Boston's *The Sunday Herald* licked their lips over this 'strange intimacy': 'what they write in these lengthy epistles no one has yet found out, but should the correspondence ever be published the Emerson-Carlyle correspondence may have to take a back seat'.[3]

Despite the evident anticipation to read the Stevenson-Barrie correspondence in the 1890s, it has only ever been partially published. While many of Stevenson's letters to Barrie appeared shortly after his death in 1894, and several more were gradually published over the course of the twentieth century, Barrie's letters to Stevenson have remained in the dark. Indeed, since the 1940s, some critics have suspected that Barrie's letters to Stevenson were lost. One of Barrie's closest friends, Denis Mackail, who wrote an early biography of Barrie in 1941, wished that 'more of the correspondence had survived' and

2. Gelett Burgess, 'Mrs R. L. Stevenson Interviewed', *The Bookman*, August (1898): 122–4 (122–3).

3. 'Barrie and Stevenson', *The Sunday Herald* (Boston), 12 August 1894, p. 27.

lamented that Barrie's letters to Samoa 'have
never been seen or heard of'.[4] The editor of the
only collection of Barrie's letters, Viola Meynell,
similarly wrote that the letters to Stevenson are
'lost or destroyed' in 1942.[5] More recently, Lisa
Chaney—author of the latest life of Barrie, *Hide-
and-Seek with Angels* (2005)—notes that 'his
letters to Stevenson appear to have been lost [...]
we are thus left to guess at their content through
Stevenson's replies'.[6] Like Mackail, Meynell and
Chaney, Barrie himself feared that his letters to
Samoa were lost; in her book, Chaney reproduces
one of Barrie's 1922 notebook entries, where he
states: 'odd that with so much of R. L. S. none of
the letters *to* him published. Perhaps not kept'.[7]

The letters *were* kept. While it is still un-
clear where Barrie's letters went directly after
Stevenson's death (they did not feature in the
Anderson Galleries auctions between 1914 and
1916, where the bulk of Stevenson's possessions
were sold),[8] it is clear that Edwin J. Beinecke—

....

4. Denis Mackail, *The Story of J. M. B.* (London: Peter Davies, 1941), p. 200.

5. Viola Meynell, 'Introduction', in *Letters of J. M. Barrie*, ed. by Viola Meynell (London: Peter Davies, 1942), pp. v–vii (p. vii).

6. Lisa Chaney, *Hide-and-Seek with Angels: A Life of J. M. Barrie* (London: Hutchinson, 2005), p. 123.

7. (cited in) Chaney, p. 123.

8. Some clues as to the journey of Barrie's letters after Stevenson's death

4

Stevenson's most devoted collector in the U.S.—
had acquired them by the late 1950s. Each of
the letters is referenced in George L. McKay's
magnificent six-volume catalogue of Beinecke's
collection that was presented to Yale University,
The Stevenson Library of Edwin J. Beinecke
(1951–64). A facsimile of Barrie's first letter to
Stevenson is even included in the fourth volume.[9]
Nevertheless, these letters have remained under
the radar, unpublished since they were penned
over 125 years ago, and the myth of their apparent
loss has endured.

This volume publishes all of Barrie's letters to
Stevenson in Samoa for the first time and reunites
them with the letters Barrie received from
Stevenson. Placed together, they finally chart
the development of this remarkable yet little-
known literary friendship. The introduction and
notes that follow are designed to help explain
why their friendship flourished, despite their
never meeting, and to analyse some of the key

may be buried in the Beinecke Rare Book & Manuscript Library's vast
trove of Edwin J. Beinecke's research notes [GEN MSS 664 Series IV].

9. Photostat copies of Barrie's letters to Stevenson are held in the
National Library of Scotland [Acc. 13917/216]. Short quotations from
Barrie's letters also feature in Frank McLynn's 1993 biography, *Robert
Louis Stevenson*, as well as in Booth and Mehew's footnotes for *The Letters
of Robert Louis Stevenson*.

themes and features of their correspondence. It was not simply their shared profession, but their respect for each other's 'genius', their experiences of Scotland, and their use of caustic irony that brought them together and prompted their lengthy epistles, which at times bear similarities to love letters. But the significance of these letters is not only that they give new insights into Barrie's and Stevenson's lives and friendship; this correspondence also had a marked influence on Barrie's writings and his activities following Stevenson's passing. Throughout his life, Barrie lamented the fact that he never met Stevenson in person—which prompted him to write a short story imagining an encounter with Stevenson in Edinburgh (Appendix 6)—and he went on to memorialise Stevenson and their friendship in several ways. Identifying and analysing these various memorials, the latter sections of this introduction demonstrate the lasting impact that their correspondence had on Barrie's life and work.

It might seem surprising that the two never met. Stevenson and Barrie were both well networked in literary circles; they were taught by the same professors at Edinburgh University, including

the Celtic and Greek scholar John Stuart Blackie and the historian David Masson; and they both contributed to Edinburgh University Union's book, *The New Amphion* (published to help raise funds for Teviot Row House) in 1886. But Stevenson (born in 1850) was ten years older than Barrie, so they were not exact contemporaries. When Barrie arrived in Edinburgh in 1878 to undertake his MA degree, Stevenson had already qualified for the Scottish bar (in 1875). They would have both been in Edinburgh at the beginning of 1879, but from mid-1879 until the end of Barrie's degree, Stevenson spent the majority of his time away from Auld Reekie, in America, Davos and the Scottish Highlands. A few years on, as Barrie was making his living in journalism and fiction writing in London, Stevenson had moved to Bournemouth (1884–87). By the time Barrie's star was on the rise in the late 1880s, Stevenson was living in the United States, and was shortly to embark on the journey that would result in his settling in Samoa. There was little opportunity for the two to be introduced.

There is, however, evidence of some written contact between Stevenson and Barrie before their friendship flourished in 1892. On the hunt for a role that the actress Maude Branscombe

could play,[10] Barrie sent a brief letter to Stevenson in 1886 asking if he had written any other plays besides *Deacon Brodie*. He also used this letter to compliment Stevenson on *Strange Case of Dr Jekyll and Mr Hyde*, which 'entranced us'.[11] There is no evidence to suggest that Stevenson responded to this letter, but he does appear to have contacted Barrie on another subject. In Letter 2 of the present volume, Barrie claims that he received a letter from Stevenson around 1884, in which Stevenson solicited information on the notorious Burke and Hare murders in Edinburgh, presumably in preparation for his story, 'The Body Snatcher', which was published in December 1884. It may have been in this letter that Stevenson expressed his view to Barrie that 'two men who had used the dreadful lavatory at Edinburgh University, though they never met, could never quite be strangers'.[12] This letter is most likely what Barrie was referring to when he told Stevenson's friend

----

10. Barrie had referenced Maude Branscombe in his book *Better Dead* (1887), noting that her 'photographs obstructed the traffic' [J. M. Barrie, *Better Dead* (London: George Allen & Unwin, 1887), p. 124].

11. This letter is held in the Beinecke Rare Book & Manuscript Library, Yale University [GEN MSS 664 Series I, box 9, folder 234].

12. In a letter to the Earl of Wemyss in 1922, Barrie claimed that Stevenson made this statement to him, although it doesn't appear in any of the letters from 1892 onwards. See *Letters of J. M. Barrie*, ed. by Viola Meynell (London: Peter Davies, 1942), p. 241.

and collaborator, William Ernest Henley, in 1889 that he had 'heard from R. L. S.'.[13]   Although Barrie treasured this early letter from Stevenson (storing it in his desk, as Letter 2 reveals), its current whereabouts is unknown.   Stevenson and Barrie were clearly aware of each other and in contact in the 1880s, but these early letters did not nourish a sustained correspondence; this only developed in 1892.

Despite the fact that they had never met or had much contact at that point, Barrie decided to include an essay on Stevenson in one of his earliest books, *An Edinburgh Eleven: Pencil Portraits from College Life* (1889), written under his pseudonym, Gavin Ogilvy. *An Edinburgh Eleven* provided sketches of famous contemporary figures associated with Edinburgh University and it helped make Barrie's name. But, within a few short years, he came to be greatly embarrassed by his portrait of Stevenson. While the essay noted that Stevenson's work had an 'indescribable charm', and described his characterisation of Alan Breck Stewart in *Kidnapped* as a 'masterpiece', Barrie also stated that Stevenson was a writer of 'little books',

....

13. *A Stevenson Library: Catalogue of a Collection of Writings by and about Robert Louis Stevenson formed by Edwin J. Beinecke*, ed. by George L. McKay, 6 vols (New Haven: Yale University Library, 1958), IV, p. 1376.

who was yet to write the 'great work'. Twisting
the knife, he wrote that Stevenson 'is still a boy
wondering what he is going to be', whose popu-
larity had made him 'complacent', and whose rep-
resentations of Scottish life and religion were superficial.[14] There was praise, but Barrie didn't pull
his punches either. A few years on, he expressed
regret over the essay's patronising comments in
his correspondence with Stevenson, imploring:
'I was a boy then' (Letter 8). Luckily for Barrie,
Stevenson doesn't appear to have taken his criti-
cisms too seriously. In Letter 6, he expresses his
desire to write a parody of Barrie's essay, and give
him 'all [his] sauce back again'. Indeed, he briefly
does this in Letter 12, where he gives some ironic
advice to Barrie: 'it is time to be done with trifling
and give us a great book'.

As their friendship developed, Barrie quickly became Stevenson's 'champion'. According to
Mackail, from the moment they entered correspondence, 'R. L. S. had passed beyond criticism'.[15] Mackail's judgement is not strictly true, as
these letters reveal: even in his final letter, Barrie
tells Stevenson that the subject of his novel *The*

14. J. M. Barrie, *An Edinburgh Eleven: Pencil Portraits from College Life*
(London: Office of the "British Weekly", 1889), pp. 97–101, 107.
15. Mackail, p. 200.

Ebb-Tide was 'hardly worth while', and he describes the characters as 'too lurid'. But Barrie certainly became Stevenson's champion, and would go on to explicitly update his thesis that Stevenson hadn't written a great work upon reading the unfinished novel, *Weir of Hermiston*. In a letter to Sidney Colvin (Stevenson's close friend, who let Barrie see the novel pre-publication), Barrie wrote: 'I have read it with a delight beyond words and with a growing pain such as I never felt when reading a book before. For it is incomparably the best thing he ever did, and it is but a noble fragment [...] here is the big book'.[16] Alluding to Stevenson's greatness, Barrie would also dub him the 'wizard of Samoa'—equating Stevenson with the 'wizard of the north', Sir Walter Scott.[17]

It was only in 1892, in the final three years of Stevenson's life, that the friendship with Barrie developed, when Stevenson and his family were settled at their Vailima estate in Samoa. In the late 1880s, Stevenson had embarked on a cruise of the South Seas from San Francisco, writing essays on life and landscape in the various islands, and

16. (cited in) E. V. Lucas, *The Colvins and Their Friends* (London: Methuen & Co., 1928), p. 248.

17. Letter from J. M. Barrie to Graham Balfour (15 January 1894) [National Library of Scotland: Acc 12669].

it was during this trip that he first encountered
Samoa. As he approached the islands by boat, he
wrote to Colvin that he was 'minded to stay not
very long in Samoa', and, upon arrival, he didn't
have the best first impression either, noting that
it was 'far less beautiful' than Tahiti, and that he
was 'not especially attracted by the people'. But
the climate clearly appealed to Stevenson, who was
frequently ill. Justifying his decision to move to
the South Seas, he told friends: 'Here I have some
real health'. Consequently, Stevenson purchased
a 314-acre estate in Samoa, which he described as
a 'paradise'. Beyond the climate, Stevenson would
have been attracted to Samoa as he was planning
to pen a book 'on the Samoan Trouble' that
would focus on the ongoing Samoan civil war and
the colonial interventions of the 'three powers'
(Germany, the United Kingdom and the United
States).[18]   While in Samoa, Stevenson didn't
just spectate these struggles; he became actively
involved in the political disputes. His letters to
The Times and his book, *A Footnote to History:
Eight Years of Trouble in Samoa* (1892), proved
deeply controversial in some quarters; indeed, his

18. *The Letters of Robert Louis Stevenson*, ed. by Bradford A. Booth and
Ernest Mehew, 8 vols (New Haven: Yale University Press, 1995), VI,
pp. 335, 345, 347, 352, 362.

critiques of colonial intervention brushed close to
new sedition regulations introduced by the British
High Commissioner for the Western Pacific,
John Thurston, which outlawed the expression of
'discontent or dissatisfaction [...] towards King
or Government of Samoa'.[19] In 1893, Stevenson
defiantly proclaimed that he would 'endure my
three months in Apia Gaol' rather than remain
mute on political scandals,[20] and he wrote to
British politicians, including Lord Rosebery, to
object to Thurston's definition of sedition.

While political efforts and writings took up
much of Stevenson's time in Samoa, he remained
an industrious novelist and short story writer,
and he became known amongst Samoans as
Tusitala (the teller of tales). Alongside writing
texts set in Scotland during his time in Samoa,
including *Catriona* (the sequel to *Kidnapped*) and
Weir of Hermiston, Stevenson also wrote texts
that reflected his growing interest in the Pacific
Islands, including 'The Beach of Falesá', and two
novels written in collaboration with his stepson,
Lloyd Osbourne: *The Ebb-Tide* and *The Wrecker*.
Stevenson's collaborations with Lloyd reflect his

19. (cited in) Joseph Farrell, *Robert Louis Stevenson in Samoa* (London:
MacLehose, 2017), p. 170.

20. *The Letters of Robert Louis Stevenson*, VIII, p. 24.

closeness to (and reliance on) his family during his time in Samoa. Stevenson lived at Vailima with his wife, Fanny, his mother, Margaret Stevenson, his stepchildren, Lloyd and Isobel, Isobel's husband, Joseph, and their son, Austin. He provides humorous depictions of family life in Samoa to Barrie in Letter 9, which reveal the irreverent but affectionate relationships between the various inhabitants of Vailima. His stepdaughter, Isobel Strong, became a particularly valuable figure for Stevenson as she served as his amanuensis, transcribing substantial sections of his novels and letters. She makes several humorous interventions in the letters to Barrie, and Stevenson joked with him that she had a 'growing conviction that she is the author of my works' (Letter 9).

When their friendship began in 1892, Barrie couldn't have been much further from Samoa— he was staying in Kirriemuir in Scotland, visiting close family members, especially his elderly mother whom he would go on to memorialise in his book, *Margaret Ogilvy*, and his sister Maggie. It was still more than ten years before *Peter Pan* (1904) would be staged, but Barrie was nevertheless a well-known writer on both sides of the Atlantic. He had recently published two popular books, *A Window in Thrums* (1889) and

The Little Minister (1891) that were both set in the fictional Scottish town of Thrums, which was a thinly veiled depiction of Kirriemuir, and Barrie would go on to write several bestsellers set in Thrums over the course of the 1890s. While Barrie was best known for writing prose when his friendship with Stevenson began, he was also starting to show his prowess in the theatre too. His first two sole-authored plays on the London stage, *Ibsen's Ghost* (1891) and *Walker, London* (1892), were successes, and he was developing a new play, *The Professor's Love Story* (1892). Barrie's move into the theatre didn't just mark the beginning of a shift in his professional life, it was also a turning point in his love life: he became infatuated with Mary Ansell, an actress who had starred in *Walker, London*, and they would marry two years later in Kirriemuir. At the point of their marriage in 1894, when Stevenson and Barrie had become very close friends, the *Edinburgh Evening News* reported that the newlyweds were planning to visit Samoa—a plan that is corroborated in the final letter of the Stevenson-Barrie correspondence.[21] Colvin also wrote to Stevenson on Barrie's prospective trip in 1894.[22]

....

21. 'Mr J. M. Barrie's Wedding', *Edinburgh Evening News*, 10 July 1894, p. 4.
22. *A Stevenson Library*, IV, p. 1314.

The fact that Barrie was seriously planning to traverse the globe to Samoa for his honeymoon, after receiving no more than eight letters from Stevenson, is testament to how quickly their bonds of friendship formed and strengthened through correspondence. They hit it off for a variety of reasons. Primarily, there was genuine mutual respect for each other's work. At first, Stevenson was drawn to Barrie as he saw an opportunity to support his junior's writing. In the first few letters, he adopts the position of a literary mentor to his 'brither Scot', giving advice on how best to develop his characters and plots. But, the more Stevenson read of Barrie, the more he came to detect real genius in his work, writing to him: 'I am a capable artist; but it begins to look to me as if you were a man of genius', while noting that some of Barrie's skills are 'beyond my frontier line' (Letter 6). Stevenson didn't just issue this praise to Barrie. In a letter to Henry James, Stevenson noted that his 'Muses Three' were Barrie, Kipling, and James himself. Expanding on Barrie, Stevenson stated: 'Barrie is a beauty, *The Little Minister* and the *Window in Thrums*, eh? Stuff in that young man; but he must see and not be too funny. Genius in him, but there's a journalist at his elbow—there's the risk. Look, what a page is the glove business in

the *Window*! knocks a man flat; that's guts, if you please'.[23] Stevenson similarly praised Barrie's 'A Tale of a Glove' chapter in *A Window in Thrums* (in which Jess—the mother of Jamie—repeatedly tries to hide his sweetheart's glove out of jealousy) in a letter to S. R. Crockett. He wrote: 'That is great literature'.[24]

Although Barrie had criticised aspects of Stevenson's writing in *An Edinburgh Eleven*, he was nevertheless deeply indebted to Stevenson's style.[25] In Letter 4, Barrie explicitly states that he emulated the 'Stevenson touch' in his novel, *The Little Minister*. Barrie defines this 'Stevenson touch' as the creation of evocative moments that leave the reader 'with a picture he can never forget', and it is a fitting description of a climactic moment in *The Little Minister*, where

23. *The Letters of Robert Louis Stevenson*, VII, p. 451.

24. *The Letters of Robert Louis Stevenson*, VIII, p. 153.

25. R. D. S. Jack, Douglas Gifford and Andrew Nash all note that some of Barrie's earliest writings were influenced by Stevenson, such as his 1887 novel *Better Dead*. Gifford also persuasively argues that Stevenson's influence is evident in Barrie's final story, *Farewell Miss Julie Logan* (1931). See Douglas Gifford, 'Barrie's Farewells: The Final Story', in *Gateway to the Modern: Resituating J. M. Barrie*, ed. by Valentina Bold and Andrew Nash (Glasgow: Association for Scottish Literary Studies, 2014), pp. 68–87; R. D. S. Jack, *Myths and the Mythmaker: A Literary Account of J. M. Barrie's Formative Years* (Amsterdam: Rodopi, 2010), p. 86; and Andrew Nash, '*Better Dead*: J. M. Barrie's First Book and the Shilling Fiction Market', *Scottish Literary Review* 7.1 (2015): 19–41 (30).

Adam Dishart's black dog appears, representing the ominous return of Margaret's negligent first husband, who is presumed dead. This chapter in *The Little Minister* also bears a 'Stevenson touch' in another sense: towards the end of the chapter, Dishart proposes tossing a knife to decide whether he or the dominie (Margaret's second husband and the father of her son) will get the child, Gavin.[26] It is a scene that is highly reminiscent of the beginning of Stevenson's *The Master of Ballantrae*, where a coin is tossed to decide which of the two Durie brothers will lay allegiance to the Jacobite or Hanoverian causes. As we shall see, Barrie's writing owes various debts to Stevenson, which perhaps explains why the contemporary novelist Donna Tartt characterises them as 'twinned' writers.[27] Aside from being influenced by Stevenson, Barrie also felt he could learn further from his friend in Samoa: responding to Stevenson's praise of his genius, Barrie modestly wrote of his 'sufficient sense to continue to sit at your feet' (Letter 8).

Besides their deep appreciation of each other's work, Barrie and Stevenson also bonded

....

26. J. M. Barrie, *The Little Minister* (London: Cassell and Company, c.1925), p. 277.

27. Donna Tartt, 'On Barrie and Stevenson', *Fairy Tale Review*, 1 (2005): 66–71 (68).

over their similar literary views (especially books they disliked). The first few letters of the correspondence are dominated by discussion on writers and writing, including Thomas Hardy's *Tess of the D'Urbervilles*, which Stevenson found 'languid and false to every fact and principle of human nature' (Letter 3). Although Barrie was a close friend of Hardy's, he too found *Tess* 'wrong-headed' (Letter 4), and he shares several jokes with Stevenson at Hardy's expense. Towards the end of the correspondence, they also bond over their similar experiences with another mutual contact, the Scottish novelist S. R. Crockett. Stevenson expressed his 'bitterness' towards Crockett (Letter 15) on account that Crockett had published compliments that Stevenson had issued to him without Stevenson's permission, to help advertise his book, *The Raiders*. Stevenson's 'endorsement' included a reference to Barrie: '"The Stickit Minister" [Crockett's first collection of stories] is out-of-doors—Barrie is within doors. By different ways ye shall attain'. This quote subtly invokes Stevenson's view that Barrie struggled to evoke nature in his writing. After complimenting 'A Tale of a Glove' in his letter to Crockett, Stevenson wrote: 'Look at his flood in the Little Minister; it is pitiful. Do you believe in

that island? No. No more do I'.[28] Barrie was glad
to hear of Stevenson's experiences with Crockett,
but he also gave Stevenson his own sauce back.
Parodying the comparison to Crockett, Barrie
wrote: 'As soon as I read *The Raiders* I knew it
was not by Stevenson. Crockett is downstairs.
Stevenson is upstairs. By different ways ye shall
attain' (Letter 16).

Being two writers who often spent a lot of
time outside of their native land, Stevenson and
Barrie also bonded over their reminiscences
of Scotland. Despite living in the South Seas,
Stevenson struggled to get Scotland out of his
head in the latter years of his life; he told Barrie
that 'my imagination so continually inhabit[s]
that cold old huddle of grey hills from which
we come' (Letter 5). He wrote to Barrie on the
intensity of his Scottish feeling, which was at
times 'erisypelitous'. He suspected that Barrie
felt similarly, and that they were both 'Scotty
Scots' (Letter 1). They bond over reconstructing
Kirriemuir and Glenogil, which Stevenson had
visited in his youth (Letters 15 and 16), and,
towards the end of the correspondence, their
use of Scots increases, which generates greater
intimacy through linguistic specificity.

28. *The Letters of Robert Louis Stevenson*, VIII, p. 153.

They also make references that require a knowledge of Scottish history, such as when Stevenson signs off Letter 5 to Barrie with the line: 'Faur ye weel, ye Bitch!' This statement is typical of their irreverent, comical writing, but it is also a reference to the eighteenth-century judge, Lord Kames, who is reported to have uttered a similar expression before his death. Tied to Scotland, Barrie and Stevenson also bond over illness. Barrie had a very serious illness in 1894 and Stevenson had wrestled with poor health throughout his life, forcing him to travel beyond Scotland to find a more appropriate climate. On hearing of Barrie's condition, Stevenson wrote: "'tis in vain they try to alarm me with their bulletins [...] I know pleurisy and pneumonia are in vain against Scotsmen who can write' (Letter 15). Particularly for Stevenson, their shared Scottishness was enticing, allowing him to express himself, his memories, and to make cultural references, freely.

As their friendship developed, they became more open with each other and shared their secrets, which helped build stronger bonds of trust. Ironically, it was their distance from each other that nourished this aspect of their friendship. Barrie could write to Stevenson in Samoa with a degree of confidence that any secrets about his

life or writing would be less likely to circulate. Stevenson encouraged Barrie to open up about his new projects using this very argument: 'Tell me about your new book. No harm in telling *me*; I am too far off to be indiscreet [...] I am rushes by the riverside, and the stream is in Babylon; breathe your secrets to me fearlessly' (Letter 6). Barrie did open up about his projects, and also his personal life. He wrote that, in Stevenson's company, he felt he could reveal 'the real JMB who has been so far carefully concealed from his "intimate friends"', and he confessed the real reason he didn't travel, which he also kept from his friends: 'I have a passion for my mother and my young sister which makes me stay at home' (Letter 8). There is something especially confessional and open about Barrie's letters to Stevenson that gives us a fuller portrait of him, as both a person and a writer.

In turn, Stevenson shared his thoughts with Barrie under strict confidence. After relating his suspicion that the German Empire planned to annex Samoa, and describing the Germans as a 'stiff-backed and sour-natured people', Stevenson told Barrie 'the whole of the above must be regarded as private—strictly private. Breathe it not in Kirriemuir, tell it not to the daughters of Dundee! What a nice extract this would make

for the daily papers!' (Letter 15). In line with Stevenson's request, when this letter was published after his death, the more salacious quotes were not included in several transcriptions.[29] Stevenson also whispers who his main literary debts are owed to in Letter 12—the Covenanting writers. Sharing such secrets and information built up trust between the two correspondents, but it also gave them deep insights into each other's thoughts and feelings. Midway through the correspondence, Stevenson wrote 'I am quite sure that I know you and quite sure that you know me' (Letter 9).

Their letter writing styles also helped nurture their friendship. Both excelled at writing playful, fun letters—'about nothing', as Stevenson states (Letter 15)—and they were able to engage in repartee fluidly. It also helped that the two writers had thick skins, in each other's company at least, allowing them to poke fun effortlessly. Consequently, an intimate, cheeky correspondence emerged, showcasing their similar personalities. Stevenson expressed his deep appreciation of

29. These quotations did not feature in Colvin's transcription of the letter for his two-volume collection, *The Letters of Robert Louis Stevenson to his Family and Friends* (1899) or his later volumes of Stevenson's letters, but he did include them in a transcription for an article in *Scribner's Magazine*; see Sidney Colvin, 'The Letters of Robert Louis Stevenson. Edited by Sidney Colvin. Life in Samoa: November, 1890–December, 1894', *Scribner's Magazine*, 26.5 (1899): 570-87 (584).

Barrie's letter writing abilities, which he believed eclipsed his own: 'you write such a very good letter and I am ashamed to exhibit myself before my junior (which you are after all) in light of the dreary idiot I feel' (Letter 15). But this is a modest statement: the correspondence reveals two gifted letter writers, whose corresponding styles facilitated a close bond.

Before long, Barrie considered Stevenson not only as a friend but as family. He refers to the Vailima estate as *'my household'* (Letter 10) and its inhabitants as his 'cousins' (Letter 13). To help style himself as a member of the Stevenson family, who each had native Samoan names, Barrie decided to give himself one—Softy Softy.[30] Barrie also expressed his love for Stevenson in ways that resemble the nineteenth-century tradition of romantic friendship, where close friendships were communicated in the same terms as romantic love.[31] Upon hearing that Stevenson had fallen

....

30. Barrie kept up several connections with the Vailima family after Stevenson died: he exchanged letters with Margaret, Lloyd, Graham and Austin, and he also seconded Lloyd's membership of the Garrick Club in 1914 [*A Stevenson Library*, IV, p. 1531]. Fanny visited Barrie at his country house in Farnham, Surrey on several occasions during her trip to England in 1907 [Nellie Van de Grift Sanchez, *The Life of Mrs. Robert Louis Stevenson* (New York: Charles Scribner's Sons, 1920), p. 292].

31. For more on the history of romantic friendship, see Carolyn Oulton,

seriously ill, Barrie wrote to Stevenson: 'to be blunt I have discovered (have suspected it for some time) that I love you, and if you had been a woman—' (a sentence that is teasingly left unfinished). The literary critic and folklorist Andrew Lang later noted that 'Stevenson possessed more than any man I ever met, the power of making other men fall in love with him', and, despite never meeting, Barrie was clearly susceptible to his charms too.[32] Through invoking fraternal, familial and romantic bonds, Barrie demonstrated how deep his affection for Stevenson was.

Even from the earliest stages of the correspondence, Stevenson and Barrie were keen to meet in person. Barrie signed off an early epistle: 'I wish I was this letter now that I might see you in the flesh. That I hope may be managed some day' (Letter 2). Likewise, Stevenson was determined to get Barrie to Samoa. In the initial few letters, he makes intermittent statements that encourage Barrie to visit—'we would have some grand cracks!' (Letter 6)—and these become more frequent

Romantic Friendship in Victorian Literature (London: Routledge, 2016).

32.. Andrew Lang, 'Recollections of Robert Louis Stevenson', *The North American Review*, 160 (1895): 185–94 (191–2).

and insistent as the correspondence develops. In Letter 12, Stevenson's family collectively cry, 'Come to Vailima!', and later, upon hearing that Barrie had married Mary Ansell, he demands that she 'Take and Bring you to Vailima' (Letter 15). He also provides sketches of the various residents of Vailima to 'prepare' Barrie for his visit, and lures him with the prospect of alcohol-fuelled merriment. Upon Barrie's arrival, 'the fatted bottle should be immediately slain in the halls of Vailima' (Letter 15). As we have encountered, Barrie sincerely planned to make Samoa his honeymoon location, which was reported in the Edinburgh press, but he decided against it because his mother was frail and 'so doleful at the thought of my going so far away' (Letter 16).

While *they* couldn't travel to Scotland or Samoa, smaller gifts and local wares could. Stevenson and Barrie sent photographs of themselves and their family to each other; Barrie sent fabrics from Kirriemuir, as well as a flower for Isobel; and decorated Samoan mulberry bark was sent to Barrie. These strips of mulberry bark were used to adorn Barrie's flats in the Adelphi and, according to Mackail, they were still there when Barrie died in 1937.[33] Barrie also sent editions

33. Mackail, p. 200.

of his books to Samoa, and one, a limited edition of *A Window in Thrums*, features an elaborate inscription, where Barrie comically represents the influence of Stevenson's *The Master of Ballantrae* on the inhabitants of Thrums:

> To Robert Louis Stevenson,
> from his friend J. M. Barrie

> It is common knowledge that when the dominie was coming on for eighty years he walked fifteen miles namely to Tilliedrum, to buy a book called 'The Master of Ballantrae', the which he read aloud to his scholars when they should have been at their arithmetic. On the readings being finished he demanded of them the moral of the work, to which they made correct answers, and then adjourned to the water side, where they lit two candle ends and then each fell upon his brother and pummelled him. Waster Lunny says that on the dominie's interfering he was received with cries of "Square Toes".[34]

The final two sentences here refer to Chapter 5

....

34. This inscribed copy of *A Window in Thrums* is housed in the Beinecke Rare Book & Manuscript Library [item number 7214]. A facsimile of this inscription also appears in *A Stevenson Library*, VI, facing p. 2417.

in *The Master of Ballantrae* where James and
Henry Durie fight and 'Square-Toes' (Ephraim
Mackellar) takes two candlesticks to the duel
to provide light. While Barrie provided witty
inscriptions, Stevenson's works were also embel-
lished for Barrie. Letter 9 features a headpiece
illustration by Isobel Strong, which depicts
Stevenson lying in bed reading a book, the
'Complete Works' of 'J. M. Barrie'.[35] In the absence of meeting, the two writers could bring their
worlds closer together through such attentive gifts.

They could also rely on various conduits to
give them more information about their friend.
The actress Marie Fraser, who had played in
Barrie's drama *Richard Savage* in 1891, acted
Barrie out for Stevenson when she visited Samoa
in 1892. Following this performance, Stevenson
told Barrie: 'I must say I feel as if I rather knew
you myself' (Letter 6). Barrie also got deeper
glimpses of his friend through Stevenson's
family members who travelled back to Britain.
Stevenson told Barrie that 'you may elicit all
the information you can possibly wish to have
as to us and ours' (Letter 12) from his cousin

....

35. This illustration was reproduced in Bradford A. Booth's edition of
Letter 9, *R. L. S. to J. M. Barrie: A Vailima Portrait* (San Francisco: The
Book Club of California, 1962), p. 3.

Graham Balfour, who had spent time in Vailima. In Letter 13, Barrie relates his determination to locate Balfour, despite them always missing each other. Barrie had better luck with Stevenson's mother, who had gone back to Scotland in the early months of 1893 and stayed for a year. She had a two-hour visit from Barrie in January 1894 and gave him detailed information about the Vailima household.[36] Stevenson and Barrie also heard more of each other from their mutual friends. Lang, for instance, wrote to Stevenson in 1894 and characterised Barrie as 'a weird looking little cove': 'he is not what you call a lady's man: he looks like a changeling. I like the changeling'.[37]

Electing each other and their family members to societies that they were part of was another way of developing deeper associations, even if these elections were largely ironic. For instance, Stevenson and his family 'unanimously elected' Barrie as an Ordinary Member to their playful Temperance Society for the Consumption of Whiskey Punch,[38] while Barrie elects Lloyd to

36. *The Letters of Robert Louis Stevenson*, VIII, p. 258.

37. *Dear Stevenson: Letters from Andrew Lang to Robert Louis Stevenson, with five letters from Stevenson to Lang*, ed. by Marysa Demoor (Leuven: Uitgeverij Peeters, 1990), pp. 143–4.

38. *Catalogue of Valuable Books, Autograph Letters and Manuscripts etc., comprising The Property of the late Sir J. M. Barrie* (London: Sotheby & Co., 1937), p. 20.

his famous cricketing club, the Allahakbarries, of which various famous writers were members (including Arthur Conan Doyle, Rudyard Kipling and A. A. Milne). By various means, they tried to create as much society between them as possible, despite being separated by nearly ten thousand miles.

But gifts, memberships, and accounts of each other from friends and family didn't satisfy their desire to meet. Fortunately, as creative writers, they had a further trick up their sleeve. One of the most imaginative ways they overcame their inability to meet was to write fictive scenarios in which they could interact. As one of Barrie's early biographers J. A. Hammerton wrote, 'romantics command means of intercourse that defy time and space',[39] and Stevenson and Barrie defied distance by crafting imagined meetings in their letters. One of the most striking imaginative encounters appears in Letter 8, in which Barrie includes a playlet in four Acts that represents him visiting Vailima. In this self-deprecating piece, Barrie portrays himself as a surly grouch that Louis and Fanny can't wait to be rid of. An exasperated Fanny closes the playlet, pitying

....

39. J. A. Hammerton, *Barrie: The Story of a Genius* (London: Sampson Low, Marston & Co., 1929), p. 92.

any future spouse of Barrie's: 'What if he were to marry!' Stevenson reciprocated in developing this imagined encounter. In the following letter, he envisages Isobel Strong arranging Barrie's hair and provides an alternative portrait of Fanny after Barrie's imaginary departure. In Stevenson's rendition, Fanny states: 'I like Mr. Barrie. I don't like anybody else'.

This playlet was not the only example of Barrie using the letters to imaginatively transport himself to Vailima. He relates dreams where he visits Samoa (Letter 13) and also transcribes imagined conversations between the residents of Vailima, such as their responses to his getting married (Letter 16). Barrie fancies Stevenson and his family are concerned by how he has come to know so much of Vailima. The fictional Stevenson in these conversations muses 'has my Brownie gone to Thrums!' and Isobel suspects 'Graham Balfour has been telling him things' (Letter 13). Through these imagined encounters and projections into Vailima, Barrie came to feel incredibly close to the Stevenson family. Over a decade after Stevenson's death, Barrie would remark to Isobel's son, Austin Strong, 'I feel as if I remembered Vailima about as well as you'.[40]

....

40. *A Stevenson Library*, IV, p. 1213.

Barrie didn't just like to imagine meeting with Stevenson; he also uses the letters to suggest how his characters and Stevenson's characters might interact or be related. In Letter 13, Barrie includes a striking family tree for his characters in *The Little Minister*, which demonstrates that they descended from Stevenson's characters in *Catriona*. In the tree, Barrie imagines that Babbie's great-great-grandmother is Catriona, and he envisages Babbie's and Gavin's children as named after the characters in *Catriona*, including 'Alan Dishart' and 'David B. Dishart'. Stevenson authenticates this zone of contact that Barrie constructs, telling him that his 'genealogy is no doubt quite exact' (Letter 14). As we shall see below, Barrie would later create further proximities between his and Stevenson's characters, such as in *Peter Pan*, where Barrie's characters refer to the pirates in Stevenson's *Treasure Island*. In Barrie's hands, both authors' characters could occupy the same imaginative world, and the line between fiction and reality is rarely strong. For instance, Barrie tells Stevenson that one of the protagonists in *Kidnapped*, Alan Breck Stewart, is a patron of the Allahakbarries (Letter 10). Barrie may not have met Stevenson in person, but he created numerous imagined meetings with Stevenson and

Stevenson's characters—meetings that he would continue to develop after Stevenson's death.

In his letter to Stevenson dated 11 October 1894, Barrie closes on a poignant note, identifying the Vailima household as 'the only family in the world, outside my own relations, with whom I have a close tie'. He also stresses how hard it is to close a letter to his friend in Samoa: 'I feel sorrowful when I end up, it is always saying goodbye to you for a long time'. Barrie was not to know that this sombre farewell would be his final goodbye to Stevenson. Less than two months later, Stevenson died on 3 December 1894, aged 44. Barrie had joked with Stevenson that the only fitting way for the author of *Treasure Island* to die was to walk the plank (Letter 4), but Stevenson met his end in the most domestic of settings. While making mayonnaise with Fanny in Samoa, he clutched his head and fell to the ground, most likely suffering from a brain haemorrhage and dying a few hours later. The following day, his body was taken to the top of Mount Vaea in Samoa where he was buried and a tombstone was later installed at the site, bearing the following quotation from his poem 'Requiem':

Here he lies where he longed to be;
Home is the sailor, home from the sea,
And the hunter home from the hill.

Barrie was not only distraught upon hearing the news of Stevenson's death, but confused: he received word via telegram that Stevenson had died of 'asalad' and had no idea what this could mean. It was soon clarified that Stevenson had died while making 'a salad'.[41]

Barrie's response to Stevenson's death was twofold: he experienced deep regret at having never met his friend in person, a feeling that would resurface throughout his life, but also a determination to commemorate Stevenson's life, his writing and their friendship. As the Appendices of this volume demonstrate, Barrie commemorated Stevenson in various ways after his death: writing poetry and prose on Stevenson, stressing the debt his own writing owed to him and their correspondence, and even helping to establish public monuments in Stevenson's honour. These memorials are testament to the influence that the Stevenson-Barrie correspondence had upon Barrie's life and artistic development.

41. *Letters of J. M. Barrie*, p. 231.

Barrie's desire to commemorate Stevenson's life was expressed just days after his friend's death. Within weeks of Stevenson's death, he had published a poem, 'Scotland's Lament' (Appendix 1), which appeared in *The Bookman* in early 1895. The poem focuses on Stevenson's mother, and through his depiction of her, Barrie was able to express his own grief, as well as the nation's. Indeed, the mother figure who emerges in 'Scotland's Lament' is less Margaret Stevenson and more a 'mother of the nation' figure, a Caledonia, whose sons include Walter Scott, Robert Burns and, naturally, Stevenson himself. The first four stanzas reveal Barrie's interest in expressing how he and the nation share a mother's grief:

Her hands about her brows are pressed,
She goes upon her knees to pray,
Her head is bowed upon her breast,
And oh, she's sairly failed the day!

Her breast is old, it will not rise,
Her tearless sobs in anguish choke,
God put His finger on her eyes,
And then it was her tears that spoke.

"I've ha'en o' brawer sons a flow,
My Walter mair renown could win,
And he that followed at the plough,
But Louis was my Benjamin![42]

"Ye sons wha do your little best,
Ye writing Scots, put by the pen,
He's deid, the ane abune the rest,
I winna look at write again!"

An extremely personal expression of grief, contemporary critics treated the poem's sentimentality harshly. The *Edinburgh Evening News*, for instance, labelled the poem 'wailing gibberish' and described the mother figure as a 'dotard and a driveller'. *Caledonia*, a literary magazine, was more forgiving, but it noted that only six of the seventeen stanzas were worthy of praise: the first three, the thirteenth and the final two.[43] Despite this disappointing reception, the poem is revealing of Barrie's feelings towards Stevenson. For instance, we hear Barrie's own voice coming through in the fourth stanza quoted,

42. Benjamin, who Stevenson is correlated to, was the youngest son of Jacob.

43. Alexander Lowson, 'Echoes from the Sanctum', *Caledonia: A Monthly Magazine* (Aberdeen: W. Jolly & Sons, 1895), pp. 187–92 (pp. 190–1).

when the mother states that no living Scottish writer can equal Stevenson. In one of his early letters to Stevenson (Letter 2), Barrie suggests he might as well give up writing after encountering the brilliance of the early chapters of Stevenson's *The Master of Ballantrae* (1889). Indeed, Barrie repeated this sentiment in his book *Margaret Ogilvy* (1896), a biography of his own mother, in which he states that he 'saw no use in ever trying to write again' after reading this same work of Stevenson's (Appendix 5). Thus the mother's grief in 'Scotland's Lament' can be considered a proxy for Barrie's, as well as Scotland's and Margaret Stevenson's.

The two writers' correspondence also informs these stanzas in another way. In Stevenson's final letter to Barrie, when encouraging his friend to visit him in Samoa, Stevenson wrote: 'I tell you frankly you had better come soon. I am sair failed a'ready; and what I may be if you continue to dally, I dread to conceive'. Barrie clearly incorporates the expression 'sair failed' (severely frail) into the first stanza of 'Scotland's Lament'. The fact that Barrie was concentrating on a line from Stevenson's final letter, where Stevenson highlighted just how infirm he was because Barrie hadn't yet visited, reflects the regret (and perhaps

guilt) Barrie felt at not having made the visit to Samoa. The echoes of the Barrie-Stevenson correspondence in 'Scotland's Lament' add further meaning to the poem: it is not simply a national memorial or a meditation on Margaret Stevenson's loss, but a memorial to Barrie's and Stevenson's friendship and their correspondence.

While 'Scotland's Lament' and his later commemorations took a literary form, perhaps the most enduring tribute to Stevenson that Barrie was involved in creating was the St Giles' Cathedral Memorial—a huge bas-relief sculpture in the High Kirk of Edinburgh, based on a medallion portrait of Stevenson by Augustus Saint-Gaudens, which was installed in 1904. 1904 was ten years after Stevenson's death, and that substantial length of time tells its own tale: the Stevenson memorial was controversial. In a letter to a fellow writer, Arthur Quiller-Couch, Barrie noted that while the students, the poor and the 'cultured' of Edinburgh supported the memorial, much of Edinburgh's 'influential' society were 'as they always were indifferent to R.L.S. and think this confounded "art" [the proposed memorial] an absurdity'.[44] As Philip Waller has stated, it may have been the 'lingering memories of

44. *Letters of J. M. Barrie*, pp. 11–12.

38

Stevenson's raffish and godless student days' that underpinned the resistance to a Stevenson monument amongst Edinburgh's gentility.[45] Indeed, according to Quiller-Couch, Stevenson's professors at Edinburgh University were among those most hesitant over the statue.[46] It was Lord Rosebery, the former Prime Minister, who proved a key figure in quelling these anxieties towards the memorial. As we have seen, Rosebery had been an important ally to Stevenson during his time in Samoa. Barrie had his own history with Rosebery, albeit less amicable: in an essay in *An Edinburgh Eleven* (1889), Barrie confessed to throwing 'a clod of earth' at the statesman (and missing him) during his student days at Edinburgh University, demonstrating his opposition to the House of Lords.[47] But, in 1896, Barrie praised Rosebery's courage in leading the campaign for a Stevenson memorial.

On 10 December 1896, two years after Stevenson's death, Rosebery organised a meeting at the Edinburgh Music Hall to discuss establishing a national memorial to the writer,

45. Philip Waller, *Writers, Readers and Reputations: Literary Life in Britain 1870–1918* (Oxford: Oxford University Press, 2006), p. 243.

46. A. T. Quiller-Couch, 'Mr Barrie's "Sentimental Tommy"', *The Contemporary Review*, 70 (1896): 652–62 (659).

47. J. M. Barrie, *An Edinburgh Eleven*, p. 7.

by public subscription. He spoke to a packed hall, whose audience included Stevenson's mother, and he expressed his bewilderment at the fact that 'in this age of memorials and testimonials no stone or cairn had been put up' for Stevenson. While other cities—including San Francisco—had set up committees to establish Stevenson memorials, Edinburgh, Stevenson's home city, had not. Subtly criticising those opposed to the memorial, Rosebery continued: 'I do not, at any rate, wish to belong to a generation of which it shall be said that they had this consummate being living and dying among them, and did not recognise his splendour and his merit'.[48] Barrie believed that many of the 'snobbish' critics of the memorial, as he called them, only softened their resistance because of Rosebery's involvement and his status.[49]

It wasn't Rosebery alone who helped quell these anxieties around a Stevenson memorial; Barrie's contribution was also significant. Despite personal reluctance, Barrie decided to address the audience. He confessed to Stevenson's mother, 'I am the poorest speaker, but hope my love for Louis

48. 'Robert Louis Stevenson Memorial', *The Scotsman*, 11 December 1896, p. 7.

49. *Letters of J. M. Barrie*, pp. 11–12.

will help me through'.[50] In his speech (Appendix 3), Barrie stressed that 'it was no one single class that loved Stevenson. All classes did'—although he well knew that many in the middle and upper classes of Edinburgh were less appreciative of this celebrated son. He also highlighted that Stevenson appealed to both sexes, to Americans and Polynesians as well as Europeans, and that every writer (be they Romanticist or Realist, Idealist or Pessimist) claimed and admired Stevenson:

> They all saw with different eyes, but they were all proud of Stevenson, who, beyond all other writers, was the man who showed them how to put their houses in order before they began to write, in what spirit they should write, with what aim, and with what necessity of toil [...] Stevenson was dead, but he still carried their flag, and because of him the most unworthy among them were a little more worthy, and the meanest of them a little less mean.

Barrie makes a concerted effort here to style

---

50. Letter from J. M. Barrie to Mrs Stevenson (3 December 1896) [Beinecke Rare Book & Manuscript Library. GEN MSS 1400 Series I, box 14, folder 488].

Stevenson as the most significant writer of his age—heightening the argument for a memorial—but also as a unifying figure, in a bid to isolate those opposed to the memorial. Throughout his life, Barrie struggled to understand the antipathy of some in Edinburgh to Stevenson, and he had a 'brief flare of irascibility' in 1922 when he visited the city and no one could direct him to Stevenson's house.[51]

At the end of Barrie's speech, which was loudly applauded, he proposed forming a representative committee for establishing the memorial, which was agreed on at the meeting and immediately appointed. The historian Professor David Masson was to be chairman, with Rosebery as president and Barrie serving on the executive committee. Following the formation of this committee, 17,000 copies of an appeal for subscription were sent out, to which Barrie contributed 20 guineas, making him the third-largest subscriber after Rosebery and the Edinburgh-based publisher, T & A Constable.[52] Various notaries contributed to this fund, including Hardy, Kipling, Conan Doyle

51. Cynthia Asquith, *Portrait of Barrie* (London: James Barrie, 1954), p. 68.

52. 'Third Edition,' *Freeman's Journal & Daily Commercial Advertiser*, 12 June 1897, p. 11; 'The Robert Louis Stevenson Memorial,' *The Pall Mall Gazette*, 15 July 1898, p. 8.

and Meredith, and by July 1898, £1,400 had been raised (around £80,000 today). It was decided that a sculptural mural should be installed in St Giles' Cathedral, designed by Saint-Gaudens, and it was further agreed that, should there be any money left over, a red granite seat would be placed at the top of Arthur's Seat or Calton Hill, overlooking the Firth of Forth—a memorial that would embody Stevenson's love of the sea.[53] Although the latter memorial was, regrettably, never realised, Rosebery unveiled the bas-relief in St Giles' Cathedral in 1904, where it continues to occupy a prominent position to this day.

After the memorial meeting, Barrie arranged a lunch date with Stevenson's mother (Appendix 4), whose grief he had alluded to in 'Scotland's Lament'. Both Barrie and Stevenson were close to their mothers, and in their correspondence they imagined a meeting between the two women, Margaret Stevenson and Margaret Ogilvy. Barrie wrote to Stevenson: 'We are hoping to see your mother before long here [in Kirriemuir]. She and my mother want to talk about two boys, who had hooping cough, and did other extraordinary things. I think she is delightful' (Letter 13). The idea of this meeting excited Stevenson, who

53. 'The Stevenson Memorial,' *The Standard*, 14 July 1898, p. 2.

Augustus Saint-Gaudens, Robert Louis Stevenson Memorial,
St Giles' Cathedral, Edinburgh.

From Graham Balfour's The Life of Robert Louis Stevenson
(New York: Charles Scribner's Sons, 1915), facing p. 338.

responded: 'nothing could possibly please me more than a meeting between the two mothers. The Hooping Cough is a grand subject; and will they no have their albums and press-notices to compare? A fountain of genial laughter arises at the thought', which Stevenson followed with a couplet:

> When the mithers of Alan and Ogilvy met
> The tea was untasted although it was set.

While Stevenson imagines a congenial meeting between the two mothers, Margaret Ogilvy may not have been as keen to meet the mother of Robert Louis Stevenson as he supposes. In Barrie's biography of his mother, he devotes a chapter to her relationship to Stevenson's writing, titled 'R. L. S.' (Appendix 5). Here, Barrie evokes his mother's avowed distaste for Stevenson when in company, as well as her private pleasure in his writing. *Margaret Ogilvy* was described by Hammerton as 'the most enduring memorial, the most beautiful monument, that ever sprang from filial love',[54] but the 'R. L. S.' chapter demonstrates that Barrie was not only memorialising his mother, but Stevenson as well. Indeed, Hammerton questioned whether

54. Hammerton, *Barrie: The Story of a Genius*, p. 214.

46

'so beautiful a tribute as that which is dedicated to Stevenson in the chapter of "Margaret Ogilvy" entitled "R. L. S."' had ever been written.[55]

The chapter begins with Barrie's typically sentimental but acerbic portrayal of Margaret Ogilvy:

> R. L. S. These familiar initials are, I suppose, the best beloved in recent literature, certainly they are the sweetest to me, but there was a time when my mother could not abide them. She said 'That Stevenson man' with a sneer, and it was never easy to her to sneer. At thought of him her face would become almost hard, which seems incredible, and she would knit her lips and fold her arms, and reply with a stiff 'oh' if you mentioned his aggravating name.

Barrie describes his efforts to goad his staunchly Presbyterian mother, going so far as putting the cover for a Thomas Carlyle book around his copy of *The Master of Ballantrae*, so that she picks it up (and 'skin[s]' it). However, later in

55. J. A. Hammerton, *J. M. Barrie and his Books* (London: Horace Marshall & Sons, 1900), p. 223.

the chapter, Barrie recounts noticing the copy of *Ballantrae* hidden under his mother's blanket. It transpires that the romancer, Stevenson, was one of her guilty pleasures. On another occasion, he tells us that he found her holding *Treasure Island* 'close to the ribs of the fire (because she could not spare a moment to rise and light the gas)'.[56] Barrie writes that what eventually attracted his mother to Stevenson was the fact that 'he was the spirit of boyhood tugging at the skirts of this old world of ours and compelling it to come back and play,' which echoes a line spoken by the mother figure in 'Scotland's Lament': '[he] pu'd my coats to mak me play'. *Margaret Ogilvy* is a memorial that affectionately pokes fun at Barrie's mother's gravity and loyalty while also highlighting the irresistibility of Stevenson's writings and playful spirit, even for his supposed detractors.

Although less explicit than in *Margaret Ogilvy*, Stevenson and his characters had a marked influence on Barrie's novels and plays too. The Barrie-Stevenson correspondence had a particular impact on Barrie's novel *Sentimental Tommy* (1896) and its sequel, *Tommy and Grizel*

....

56. In *An Edinburgh Eleven*, Barrie writes of a similar situation: 'Over "Treasure Island" I let my fire die in winter without knowing that I was freezing' (p. 98).

(1900), in which the young protagonist, Tommy Sandys, adopts the persona of Captain Stroke, an alias for Charles Edward Stuart. Hammerton writes that there was speculation that the novel was a study of Stevenson, an idea that he dismissed as 'too absurd to be entertained for one moment'.[57] But Letter 13 reveals that Stroke was at least partly modelled on Stevenson, an idea that amused the latter. In Letter 15, Stevenson becomes inquisitive about Captain Stroke and his end, enquiring of Barrie: 'AM I HANGIT?' This question clearly stimulated Barrie. In a later letter to Cynthia Asquith, his personal secretary, Barrie wrote that Stevenson's question inspired the ending of *Tommy and Grizel*,[58] where Tommy accidentally hangs himself. Barrie also makes subtle references to Stevenson in *Sentimental Tommy*. When Stroke arrives in Scotland to stage the 'last Jacobite Rising' (in response to Queen Victoria's birthday celebrations), he leaps off a boat named 'the *Dancing Shovel*'—a reference to Stevenson's work-in-progress, *Henry Shovel*, which Barrie had mentioned in *An Edinburgh Eleven*. A few sentences on, one of the characters welcomes

57. Hammerton, *J. M. Barrie and his Books*, p. 157.

58. *Letters of J. M. Barrie*, p. 190.

Barrie and his mother, Margaret Ogilvy, c. 1890.
Llewelyn Davies family papers.
Beinecke Rare Book & Manuscript Library,
Yale University.

Stroke and states 'there's an egg to your tea'.[59] This odd statement gains more meaning when placed alongside this correspondence: it is a reference back to Letter 15 where Stevenson advises Barrie's mother to 'add an egg to her ordinary', when discussing her breakfast and afternoon tea. As was evident with 'Scotland's Lament', Barrie was keen to weave aspects of their correspondence into his own fiction and, in this instance, we find it to have directly inspired the plot of the *Sentimental Tommy* texts, described by Lisa Chaney as Barrie's under-appreciated 'work of genius'.[60]

It is perhaps Barrie's most enduring creation, *Peter Pan*, which reveals his greatest literary debt to Stevenson. The parallels to be drawn between *Peter Pan* and Stevenson's writing are numerous.[61] For instance, Barrie very clearly suggests that the pirates of Neverland occupy the same world as those in Stevenson's *Treasure Island*: Long John Silver's aliases, Barbecue and Sea-Cook, are referenced in *Peter and Wendy* (1911), while the Walrus ship, Captain Flint and the plank walking

59. J. M. Barrie, *Sentimental Tommy* (London: Cassell and Company, 1924), p. 248.

60. Chaney, p. 129.

61. Maria Tatar's *The Annotated Peter Pan: The Centennial Edition* (New York: W. W. Norton & Company, 2011) identifies various references to Stevenson throughout *Peter and Wendy*.

in *Peter Pan* (1904) owe further debts. There are more subtle references to Stevenson's work too. In *Peter Pan in Kensington Gardens* (1906), for instance, Pan is described as being 'Betwixt-and-Between', just like David Balfour in Stevenson's *Kidnapped* (1886), while Robert Douglas-Fairhurst notes that Barrie probably had Stevenson's poem 'My Shadow' in mind when writing *Peter Pan*, the final stanza of which describes the separation of a child from its shadow.[62] Along with Stevenson's novels and poetry, his correspondence and friendship with Barrie also appear to have influenced the creation of *Peter Pan*. In *Margaret Ogilvy*, Barrie recounts Stevenson giving him whimsical directions to Samoa: 'You take the boat at San Francisco, and then my place is the second to the left'. While there is no evidence of Stevenson writing these directions in the letters—they may be one of Barrie's own imaginative embellishments—he nevertheless attributed them to Stevenson, and they seem to have inspired one of the most memorable lines of *Peter Pan*, when Pan describes where he lives. With equal vagueness, Pan points to the stars and states, 'second to the right and

62. Robert Douglas-Fairhurst, 'Introduction', in *The Collected Peter Pan*, ed. by Robert Douglas-Fairhurst (Oxford: Oxford University Press, 2019), pp. xiii–xlvi (p. xxvii).

52

then straight on till morning'.[63] This association
of Samoa with Neverland invites the question of
whether Neverland can be read as a symbol of
Samoa, and the play more broadly as a reflection
on its author's friendship with Stevenson. As we
have seen, Barrie often associated Stevenson with
the spirit of youth, a man of Neverland, and, just
as Pan feels sorrow for leaving his mother,[64] Barrie
expressed guilt at the thought of leaving his own
mother when he considered visiting Stevenson
in Samoa. It's also worth noting in this context
that Stevenson wrote an essay titled 'Pan's Pipes'
in 1878, and that Fanny was often compared to
(and loved) tiger lilies. But, while various parallels
can be drawn between Barrie's mooted trip to
Samoa and the journey to Neverland, we should
avoid reducing *Peter Pan* solely to a comment or
reflection on the relationship between the two
writers. While Stevenson, as both writer and
friend, undoubtedly informs *Peter Pan*, a range of
other writers also influence Barrie's play of ageing
and loss. It is a play with several universal themes
that draws upon particularities from its author's
life, including his friendship with Stevenson.

63. J. M. Barrie, *Peter Pan and Other Plays*, ed. by Peter Hollindale
(Oxford: Oxford University Press, 2008), p. 98. Tatar comments on this
comparison on p. 39 of *The Annotated Peter Pan*.

64. Barrie, *Peter Pan and Other Plays*, p. 132.

Barrie's final memorial to Stevenson sees him embellishing his friendship with Stevenson even further. One of Barrie's great regrets was never meeting Stevenson, and, in 1922, he decided to imaginatively remedy this situation by describing how they *might* have met in the form of a short story. That year, Barrie had contributed an entry to a collection of reminiscences about Stevenson, *I Can Remember Robert Louis Stevenson*, edited by Rosaline Masson, the daughter of Professor David Masson. Despondent upon reading his own comments when the volume was published, where he noted that he had never met Stevenson and had no right to be in the volume, Barrie wrote a follow-up letter to Masson with an alternative entry (Appendix 6), which she published in the second edition in 1925. In this second entry, Barrie offers a short story in which he imagines bumping into Stevenson on a snowy day in Edinburgh as a student. Taking notice of Stevenson's velvet coat and his dandyish appearance, Barrie gives him a look of disapproval, to which the fictional Stevenson protests, 'God made me', and Barrie replies, 'He is getting careless'. Impressed at this response, Stevenson takes the younger man by the arm, leading him away from the University towards a howff, where he pawns his

velvet coat in exchange for numerous bottles of Chambertin. The two get drunk, quarrel and sing, and the story ends with Stevenson chasing Barrie around the snowy streets of Edinburgh, shouting 'stop thief!'. Barrie's friend, the Liberal Party politician Augustine Birrell, described the story as 'a work of art. It made me laugh. It made me cry. I would have liked it to go on and on'.[65] The affectionate nature of the tale is enhanced by the fact that Barrie loosely parodies Stevenson's works throughout, including *Treasure Island* and an early story, 'A Lodging for the Night', which also features thieves, a wintry night and a reference to students getting drunk and knocking on doors. Barrie's revised entry is emblematic of his writing: playfully presenting alternative realities that reveal absence and loss in our own worlds. His final commemoration of Stevenson, it demonstrates the anguish he felt over never meeting his close friend, and pays tribute to the strength of the friendship that these two great writers built through letters.

....

65. Asquith, p. 169. Barrie also related the story at the Printers' Pension Corporation dinner in November 1924, which Birrell attended. The speech is reproduced in *M'Connachie and J. M. B*, pp. 68–74.

Note on the Text

THE LETTERS BY ROBERT LOUIS STEVENSON INCLUDED IN THIS VOLUME HAVE ALL BEEN published previously. Rather than solely rely on the transcriptions presented in Bradford A. Booth and Ernest Mehew's authoritative, eight-volume *The Letters of Robert Louis Stevenson* (Yale University Press), or those in Sidney Colvin's early collections of Stevenson's letters, I returned to the original manuscripts, where possible, to undertake my own transcriptions. This allowed me to make editorial decisions according to my own system—outlined below—and also to correct the few inaccuracies in the Booth and Mehew transcriptions, such as in Letter 15 where they transcribe 'afore' as 'for me' (repeating Colvin's mistake from his 1899 transcription). The series of letters from J. M. Barrie to Stevenson included here has never been published before, although rough, incomplete transcriptions (by an unknown transcriber) are stored alongside the manuscript

letters at the Beinecke Library. While these sheets proved useful for consultation, they were too rough and unreliable to use as a base text for this volume so I transcribed from Barrie's original manuscripts.

I have endeavoured to present faithful transcriptions of the manuscript texts, only making minor editorial interventions that ease readability. Barrie has a tendency to use short forms in his letters, such as 'cd', 'wd', 'agst', 'tho' and '&'. For clarity, I have expanded on these contractions, so they are presented here as 'could', 'would', 'against', 'though' and 'and'. I also expand on abbreviated dates, so 'Sep 25, 92' is presented as 'September 25, 1892', for instance. I have silently corrected obvious misspellings, although I do ocassionally draw attention to these in footnotes, such as in Letter 3 when Isobel Strong (Stevenson's amanuensis) spells 'Barrie' as 'Barry', which prompts Stevenson to write 'my amanuensis cannot spell your name' on the letter. Where the authors underline to show stress in the manuscripts, I use italics. Sometimes Barrie will underline the titles of books and, at other times, he will place them in quotation marks. I have maintained Barrie's inconsisentcy. Words that are struck through in the manuscript letters have been removed, but I include two

strikethroughs in Letter 16, as they appear to be deliberate mistakes. Isobel Strong's red-ink interventions in Stevenson's letters are preserved and appear in bold type.

Both writers occasionally write very long paragraphs, covering numerous topics, which undermine clarity and readability. Like Booth and Mehew, I introduce a paragraph break in Letter 15, beginning 'I had a very', while I also break up Barrie's very long paragraph in Letter 10, which runs over four manuscript pages, from 'Greeting' to 'ye olden time'. Where words are mistakenly repeated (such as when Stevenson writes 'I am told that that it was' in Letter 12), I have corrected the mistake. Regarding quotation marks at the end of sentences, both Stevenson and Barrie are inconsistent in their placement: sometimes the full stop appears inside the quotation, sometimes outside, and sometimes it is impossible to tell. As full stops appear inside quotation marks more frequently, I have made this consistent throughout.

In Letter 14, Stevenson writes that Barrie had the second-worst handwriting he had ever encountered. I (and several friends, family members and colleagues) have shared Stevenson's frustration at times, and there remain two words that I have niggling doubts over: 'gun' in Letter 4 and 'Some'

in Letter 13. Rather than include a bracketed question mark in these instances, I put these words forward as the best transcriptions, balancing both palaeography and context. I draw attention to them by highlighting in the footnotes that Barrie's handwriting is particularly opaque in these cases.

Where diagrams feature in the letters, every effort has been made to reproduce their format as faithfully as possible within the limits of typography. In such instances, I include a reproduction of the manuscript page featuring the diagram to bring full clarity.

As for the selection of the material that features, I wanted the volume to focus on the emergence of their friendship from 1892 and its afterlife, so I chose not to include some documents that are ancillary to that focus. For instance, I have not included Barrie's short letter to Stevenson from 1886 where he praises *Jekyll and Hyde*—a letter that Stevenson does not appear to have responded to. I also haven't included Barrie's essay on Stevenson from *An Edinburgh Eleven* (1889) in the Appendices as it was written before their friendship began. Instead, I discuss these documents in the introduction as they provide relevant background contexts to the emergence of their sustained correspondence. The *Edinburgh Eleven* essay is freely and easily accessible online.

The letters are arranged chronologically to replicate the interchange of letters. Stevenson does not always date his letters so I provide rough dates in brackets in these cases, drawing on Booth and Mehew's research as well as biographical details. Their letters were often accompanied with gifts and photographs so the inclusion of several images in this volume hopes to evoke these material and visual aspects of the correspondence. The six appendices are roughly chronological and they chart the development of Barrie's memorials to Stevenson from the 1890s to the 1920s.

The Letters

1

Vailima, Samoa

[c. 18] February 1892

Dear Mr Barrie,

This is at least the third letter I have written you,
but my correspondence has a bad habit of not
getting so far as the post. That which I possess
of manhood turns pale before the business of
the address and envelope. But I hope to be more
fortunate with this: for, besides the usual and
often recurrent desire to thank you for your
work—you are one of four that have come to the
front since I was watching and had a corner of
my own to watch,[1] and there is no reason, unless
it be in these mysterious tides that ebb and flow,
and make and mar and murder the works of poor
scribblers, why you should not do work of the best
order. The tides have borne away my sentence,
of which I was weary at any rate, and between
authors, I may allow myself so much freedom as

1. It is not entirely clear who the three other writers that Stevenson refers
to here are, although Rudyard Kipling was most likely one of them.

to leave it pending. We are both Scots besides, and I suspect both rather Scotty Scots; my own Scotchness tends to intermittency, but is at times erisypelitous[2]—if that be rightly spelt. Lastly, I have gathered we had both made our stages in the metropolis of the winds: our Virgil's "grey metropolis," and I count that a lasting bond. No place so brands a man.[3]

Finally, I feel it a sort of duty to you to report progress. This may be an error, but I believed I detected your hand in an article—it may be an illusion, it may have been by one of those industrious insects who catch up and reproduce the handling of each emergent man—but I'll still hope it was yours—and hope it may please you to hear that the continuation of *Kidnapped* is under way.[4] I have not yet got to Alan, so I do not know

....

2. Erysipelas is a potentially serious bacterial infection.

3. The 'grey metropolis' referenced here is Edinburgh. Stevenson was born, raised and educated in Edinburgh, and, like Barrie, he had been a student at Edinburgh University. Both men wrote non-fiction books on Edinburgh: Stevenson published a series of essays on Edinburgh's geography and history, *Edinburgh: Picturesque Notes* (1878), and Barrie wrote *An Edinburgh Eleven* (1889), which provides biographical accounts of eleven contemporaries (one of which was Stevenson).

4. According to Booth and Mehew, this is a reference to Barrie's article 'My Favourite Magazine', published in the *British Weekly* on 20 August 1891, under Barrie's pseudonym Gavin Ogilvy [*The Letters of Robert Louis Stevenson*, VII, p. 238]. Here, Barrie calls for a new literary magazine, one that would publish 'The Further Remarkable

if he is still alive, but David seems to have a kick or two in his shanks. I was pleased to see how the Anglo-Saxon theory fell into the trap: I gave my Lowlander a Gaelic name, and even commented on the fact in the text; yet almost all critics recognised in David and Alan a Saxon and a Celt. I know not about England; in Scotland at least, where Gaelic was spoken in Fife little over the century ago, and in Galloway not much earlier, I deny there exists such a thing as a pure Saxon, and I think it more than questionable if there be such a thing as a pure Celt.[5]

But what have you to do with this? and what have I? Let us continue to inscribe our little bits of tales, and let the heathen rage!—Yours, with sincere interest in your career,

Robert Louis Stevenson

....

Adventures of Alan Breck' (in other words, a sequel to *Kidnapped*). Barrie's wish was fulfilled: Stevenson published *Catriona* in 1893.

5. For more on Stevenson's interest in Celtic and Saxon identity in Scotland, see Julia Reid's *Robert Louis Stevenson, Science, and the Fin de Siècle* (Houndmills: Palgrave Macmillan, 2006), pp. 129, 158.

2

Kirriemuir
Scotland

May 8, 1892[1]

Dear Mr Stevenson,

I was more than very glad to have your letter.
You are not aware that it is the second.[2] The first
is in the desk I am writing on—an eight year old
letter that gave me mighty pleasure at the time,
though the subject was only Messrs. Burke and
Hare.[3] In London later I had romantic schemes
for getting inside your walls at Bournemouth—
so vivid that I still feel as if they had come off.[4]

1. Although this letter is dated 8 May 1891, it is very clearly a response
made to Stevenson's previous letter from February 1892. Barrie himself
notes in Letter 8 that he sent this letter on the day he found out that
James Winter, the fiancé of his sister, Margaret ('Maggie'), had died,
which was 8 May 1892. Tragically, Winter was flung from a horse that
Barrie had gifted to him.

2. The whereabouts of this letter from Stevenson to Barrie from around
1884 (if it still exists) is unknown.

3. In 1884, Stevenson penned a short story on Burke and Hare, titled
'The Body Snatcher'. It was first published in the *Pall Mall Gazette*
'Christmas extra' in December 1884.

4. Between 1884 and 1887, Stevenson lived in Bournemouth with his
wife, Fanny, in a house called Skerryvore, named after the great light-

One, I remember, was to shoot black arrows (with couplets) at your windows, and another was to startle you in the still night by the sound of a stick that might be Pew's coming nearer and nearer.[5]

Curiously enough I don't know if I did write this article you speak of. If it appeared some time ago, I did. That is to say I have written a good many articles or the like calling for the continuation of "Kidnapped", but have written no articles at all for the last year. That it is on the way at last is fine news to me, but don't kill Alan or we shall all be sulky, i.e. if he is dead at the start. Meanwhile, I think the "Master of Ballantrae" the best thing you have done—I mean the Scotch part of it only. I felt when reading it that the rest of us had better go and turn ploughmen. The second half, however, seemed to me not worth your while.[6] This is a

house built off the west coast of Scotland by the Stevenson family firm.

5. Pew and the 'black arrows' are references to Stevenson novels: Blind Pew is one of the most fearsome characters in *Treasure Island* (1883), and Stevenson wrote a novel titled *The Black Arrow* in 1883.

6. Various different locations are charted in *The Master of Ballantrae*, including Scotland, France, India and New York. The novel's action begins in Scotland and culminates in the wilderness of North America. In his review of *Ballantrae* for the *British Weekly* (1 November 1889), Barrie notes that the ending reduced the novel to a 'shocker' [(cited in), Paul Maixner 'Introduction', in *Robert Louis Stevenson: The*

quiet little place I write from, the place I call Thrums, where I live half the year and go like a clock.[7] Conan Doyle, whose work you may know, was here lately (taking amateur photographs— spent most of his time developing them in the pantry) and we were making up a list of the best short stories in English.[8] Very unscientific, we gave no writer more than one, but I wonder how they strike you. Here they are, not in any order of merit: Bret Harte's "Tennessee's Partner", Scott's "Wandering Willie's Tale", your own "Pavilion on the Links", Kipling's "Man Who Would be King", Hardy's "Three Strangers", Lytton's "Haunters and the Haunted", Q's "Old

....

Critical Heritage, ed. by Paul Maixner (London: Routledge, 1981), p. 34].

7. Barrie referred to his hometown, Kirriemuir, as 'Thrums' in his fiction. 'Thrums' is a fitting alias for a weaving town like Kirriemuir given thrums are the threads left on a weaving loom after cloth has been removed.

8. The author of the Sherlock Holmes stories became a close friend of Barrie's and visited him in Kirriemuir over Easter 1892. They were both cricket fanatics and Conan Doyle was part of Barrie's cricketing team, affectionately known as the Allahakbarries (referenced in Letter 10). Together, they wrote an unsuccessful opera, *Jane Annie*, in 1893. Conan Doyle also had a correspondence with Stevenson around the same time as the Barrie-Stevenson correspondence. In one letter, Stevenson wrote of his suspicion that Sherlock Holmes was based on Stevenson's friend and Conan Doyle's medical professor at Edinburgh University, Joseph Bell (1837–1911), which Conan Doyle confirmed in his response [Letter from Arthur Conan Doyle to Robert Louis Stevenson (30 May 1893). Beinecke Library GEN MSS 664 Series I, box 12, folder 304].

Aeson."[9] I suppose there should be a Dickens.
Meredith's "Chloe" is not quite what one means
by a short story. I am at Box Hill sometimes,[10]
and there is a good deal of talk about you in
the "chalet." I wish I was this letter now that I
might see you in the flesh. That I hope may be
managed some day.

Yours very truly

J. M. Barrie

....

9. 'Q' is a reference to Barrie's close friend Arthur Quiller-Couch, who
often published under the pseudonym, Q. Following Stevenson's death,
Quiller-Couch endeavoured to complete one of Stevenson's unfinished
novels, St Ives, and published it in 1898.

10. Flint Cottage, Box Hill, Surrey was the home of George Meredith,
which Stevenson had visited on several occasions between 1878 and
1886. Barrie, Conan Doyle and Quiller-Couch visited Box Hill in
March 1892. Barrie would go on to write a short pamphlet, titled
George Meredith 1909, upon the author's death. Meredith had a writing
chalet in the garden.

3

Vailima Plantation
Upolu, Samoa

June 20th 1892

Dear Mr Barrie,[1]

The singular fact that I should ever have been
your correspondent before this is only equalled by
the singularity of the subject on which I seem to
have chosen to correspond; and yet there seems
to hang in my memory some hazy recollection
of writing to somebody about Burke and
Hare. What I had to say upon the grisly topic I
have no guess.

One thing however is certain, I have never
before written to the author of "The Little
Minister."[2] Let me save my conscience in the

....

1. Isobel Strong, Stevenson's stepdaughter and amanuensis, had
originally spelt Barrie's name 'Mr Barry', which Stevenson corrected.
At the top of the manuscript, Stevenson writes: 'My amanuensis
cannot spell your name. R.L.S.'

2. *The Little Minister* (1891) was one of Barrie's most popular and
critically acclaimed books. Set against the context of Chartist protest,
the novel concerns Gavin Dishart, a minister who is assigned to the
Auld Licht Kirk in Thrums (a more Calvinistic faction than the 'New

beginning and assure you how profoundly I
disbelieve your complaisant statements in the
last chapter.[3] Gavin had a devil of a time with
his wife from about six weeks after the marriage
until they separated (see report of Dishart v.
Dishart in the Scotsman newspaper and Bell's
Reports).[4] So much conceded to truth I wish I
could try to make you understand with what an
exceptional keenness of pleasure I in particular
have read your beautiful story. I say "I in
particular" because it was a competition in my
family which of us should have liked it best. Your
"Little Minister" and Anstey's "Pariah" are books
we have had the luck to receive lately and which
have made the subjects of many conversations.[5]
It was a pleasant thought to me, the pleasure of
which you are too young to understand, that both

Lichts'), where he falls in love with Babbie, who was born a gypsy but
is now engaged to her guardian, Lord Rintoul. The novel addresses the
question of bigamy, as well as a theme that recurs in Barrie's works: the
complexity of mother-son relationships.

3. In the final chapter of *The Little Minister*, we are told that Gavin
and Babbie get married, have several children, and the narrator
(the dominie, or school master) states that he 'lived to rejoice in the
happiness of Gavin and Babbie' (p. 340).

4. Stevenson imagines Gavin and Babbie as historic figures who, in
reality, separated. Bell's Reports is a reference to a series of nineteenth-
century legal reports on trials in Scotland.

5. *The Pariah* (1889) by Thomas Anstey Guthrie was published under
the pseudonym 'F Anstey'.

of these were by my juniors in the art, nor was it much less pleasant that one of them should be by a brither Scot. Both Gavin and his mother are delightful, ditto the girl, and I took a great deal of pleasure, perhaps unjustifiable, in the policeman. Let me suggest to you that there was a point which it was requisite you should have worked out more fully. The situation of your heroine was very strange, its possibility depended upon the character of Lord Rintoul, and you have been content to leave his lordship a lay figure perfectly unrealised and extremely imperfectly credible. Doubtless had you followed his lordship you would have had to carry us out of those pleasant fields in which your own imagination and those of your readers delight, doubtless you would have had to lessen that air as of a fairy tale which is so engaging and doubtless you will think it comes with a very ill grace from me that I should insist in any case on realism.[6] But your story stands on the psychology of Lord Rintoul. You have not given us that psychology; *ergo*, you have not told your story.

You will think me a very dreary fellow, and a pickthank of the first water to be thus finding

6. Stevenson was a harsh critic of realism in literature, which he expressed in several essays, including 'A Gossip on Romance' and 'A Humble Remonstrance' (a response to his friend, Henry James).

fault with what has given me so much pleasure—
and both as a Scotchman and a man of English
letters—so much pride. It is just for that reason.
Forgive me my sermon and prove your forgiveness
by giving us, as soon as it is ripe, another tale as
good, or half as good as "The Little Minister."

I have always thought it was one of the
hardest parts of the fate of the man of letters
that he has so few books he can read. Even
Hardy has failed me this last time, "Tess of the
D'Urbervilles" being, as far as I could read in
it, so unaffectedly languid and false to every
fact and principle of human nature that Hardy
will require to regain his character in at least
two works before I can forgive him.[7] Since the
"Little Minister" your books will be one of those
occasional pleasures to which I look forward with
I wish you could believe how much eagerness. I
dare say you, like what I hear of all the rest of
England, have accepted "Tess." I wish I could
give you the proper cure. If you could only read
your own love scenes in the "Little Minister" you
would find in them so much more love as would
persuade you of the hollowness and falsity of the

7. Stevenson went even further in his criticism of *Tess* in a letter to
Henry James, noting that '*Tess* is one of the worst, weakest, least sane,
most *voulu* books I have yet read' [*The Letters of Robert Louis Stevenson*,
VII, p. 450].

other. But there is the trouble—we cannot read our own books, and there are at least two of mine that I would give thirty shillings to be able to peruse, for I have an idea they would amuse me.

Your grateful confrère
Robert Louis Stevenson

4

Garrick Club
W.C.[1]

September 25, 1892

Dear Mr Stevenson,

I wonder if you can quite realise the joy with
which I heard that the "Little Minister" had
passed muster in your household at Samoa. As
for the earl, I never brought him on (you will see
from my phraseology that I am writing for the
stage) without first kicking him round the room.
I told Meredith your criticism of the end, and he
(dagont) agreed with it. I refer you to a chapter
in the book where it is hinted that if Babbie
broke out after marriage Gavin was capable
of taking a stick to her (that is for men only).[2]
However I admit that as the story was originally
planned the last chapter was to be headed "The

1. In 1890, Barrie joined the Garrick Club, a gentleman's club in London
that attracted several theatrical and literary figures [Chaney, p. 83].

2. When defining her ideal man at the end of Chapter 19 of *The Little
Minister*, Babbie states that she would like a man who would 'compel
me to do his bidding; yes, even thrash me if—'. Gavin responds: 'I am
that man!' (p. 158).

Garrick Club
W.C.

Sep 25 . 52   '92

Dear Mr Stevenson

I wonder if you can
finds realise the joy with
which I heard that the "Ball.
Minister" had passed much in
ye home total at Samoa. As for
the earl, I never brought him
on (you will see from my
phraseology that) I am waiting for the
stage) without find kicking him
round the room. I told Meredith
your intention of the end, and he
(dagont) agreed with it. I nefers
for L a chapter on the

Barrie

First page of Letter 4. Edwin J. Beinecke Collection of
Robert Louis Stevenson.
Beinecke Rare Book & Manuscript Library, Yale University.

little minister is stoned out of Thrums."[3] I
had not the heart for it, but henceforth will be
relentless. Another admission, I prided myself
on having a "Stevenson touch"—where the
dominie at his desk suddenly sees the dog—but
nobody has noticed, not even yourself.[4]

If you want to know what the Stevenson
touch at its highest is, read that incident in "The
Wrecker" (called "The Wreckers") where the
gentleman with wine in him has such delightful
expressions when looking for his room.[5] There
is magic in that, and no other could have written
it since the world began. Also the end of "The
Bottle Imp."[6] It leaves one with a picture he can
never forget. The college for teaching young
Americans how to diddle each other opens up

3. At the end of Chapter 24 of *The Little Minister*, one character, Micah,
notes that 'they'll stane the minister out o' Thrums' if they hear about
his relationship with Babbie (p. 192).

4. In Chapter 36 of *The Little Minister*, Adam Dishart's black dog,
symbolising Dishart's return, appears at the dominie's school-house.
Adam Dishart was previously married to Margaret, Gavin's mother,
but he 'sauntered away' overseas (p. 273). After several years, presuming
him dead, Margaret married the dominie and gave birth to Gavin. The
return of Adam and his dog risks the exposure of Margaret's bigamy
and having a child with another man out of wedlock.

5. *The Wrecker* (1892) is a novel written by Stevenson in collaboration
with his stepson, Lloyd Osbourne.

6. First published in the *New York Herald*, 'The Bottle Imp' (1891) is a
short story that was later published in Stevenson's collection, *Island
Nights' Entertainments* (1893).

something new in you I think. Doyle thinks it
your best story, but I don't go that length, indeed
I am firmly convinced now that you are best
when you are Scotch. "The Lantern Bearers" is
a dream of beauty.[7]

I have never dared to tell anyone my opinion
of "Tess" but I always thought it wrong-headed,
and it is an uncommon relief to me to find
that you think so, too. What a queer mixture
of humour and want of humour is Hardy. His
villain says to Tess "Will you allow me to encircle
your waist with my arm?" Angel Clare is the
greatest prig in fiction unless it is Knight in "A
Pair of Blue Eyes." The Dairymaids seemed to
me to be comic opera figures. This is good. In
the book Angel carries the milkmaids across the
river in his arms one at a time (Hardy would like
to do this), but the paper in which it appeared
thought this improper, and made him wheel
them across in a barrow.[8] The last time Hardy
was seen in London he had shaved his beard and
was in a music hall talking learnedly of Lottie

7. 'The Lantern-Bearers' (1888), first published in *Scribner's Magazine*, is
an essay that reflects on Stevenson's childhood memories around North
Berwick, as well as the relationship between realist and romance novels.

8. Hardy's *Tess of the D'Urbervilles* was originally serialised in *The Graphic*
in 1891, featuring several edits (some sweeping) to dilute its more
controversial concerns. The un-edited edition was released in 1892.

this and Connie that to another enthusiast. Would not the best parody of Hardy be a letter from a young woman declining an offer of marriage, and then accepting it in the postscript? I think he is really a great man and so quaint at times that if I were a lady I should kiss him, than which nothing would please him better.

An actor who played in "Beau Austin" complained to me that he had thought one of the authors was not *a* Stevenson but *the* Stephenson. *The* man is a tremendous gun, I believe.[9] Perhaps you have heard of a similar mistake before, but this is genuine. I like to think that it is why the piece was played.

Don't believe that Kipling is not on his way to you.[10] He is fitting up a rakish craft and is to besiege you some night and make you walk the plank. I should be annoyed to think that you would not rather perish in that way than in any other. I hope you know and like "Q's" books. He is writing a novel with 274 leading characters, and would be finished by this time,

9. *Beau Austin* (1884) was a play co-written by Stevenson and William Ernest Henley. Barrie's handwriting is especially opaque here.

10. Stevenson had corresponded with Kipling in March 1891, and he was of the view that Kipling was planning to visit Samoa. Kipling is also known to have played with Barrie's cricket team, the 'Allahakbarries', and he succeeded Barrie as Lord Rector of St Andrews University in 1922.

only he always forgets their names and has to explore back for them.

Grant Allen is going on a lecturing tour to sneer at fiction.[11] A lady (actress) to whom I sent a play (damned), referring to it as the "enclosed play, Richard Savage" always calls it in conversation now "your enclosed play of Richard Savage."[12] Another to whom I gave "A Window in Thrums" thanked me for "my delightful book, Fingers and Thumbs." (And I was just going to propose to her).

I hear one can get money for books in India now. No doubt in time we shall find our chief public in "the teeming millions of our great dependency." Must point this out to Besant.[13]

When my first book "Auld Licht Idylls" came out I sent you a copy to America.[14] I wonder if it

....

11. Grant Allen was an author and critic who reviewed Stevenson's *A Footnote to History* in 1892. As Barrie reported in *An Edinburgh Eleven* (1889), Allen struggled to identify Stevenson's ranking amongst other great living writers.

12. J. M. Barrie and H. B. Marriott Watson's play *Richard Savage* premiered at the Criterion Theatre in London in 1891, based on the life of the eighteenth-century English poet, Richard Savage.

13. Walter Besant was a novelist who founded the Authors' Club in 1891; Barrie was an early member. Besant's lecture 'The Art of Fiction' (1884) started a literary debate that solicited many responses, including one from Stevenson—his essay, 'A Humble Remonstrance' (1884).

14. Barrie's *Auld Licht Idylls* (1888) is a series of short stories set in and around the fictional town of Thrums. An inscribed copy to Stevenson is held in the University of Delaware Library.

ever reached you. I watched the post for years.
The Auld Licht Kirk of Thrums has been taken
down to make way for another (for there is still
an old woman left), and the pulpit bought by a
native who lets you sit in it for a penny. Those
who sit have the strangest experiences.

Yours very truly,
J. M. Barrie

This is my best address.

5

Vailima Plantation, Samoan Islands

November 1st, 1892

Dear Mr Barrie,

I can scarce thank you sufficiently for your extremely amusing letter. No, *The Auld Licht Idylls* never reached me. I wish it had and I wonder extremely whether it would not be good for me to have a pennyworth of the Auld Licht pulpit. It is a singular thing that I should live here in the South Seas under conditions so new and so striking, and yet my imagination so continually inhabit that cold old huddle of grey hills from which we come. I have just finished *David Balfour*.[1] I have another book on the stocks, *The Young Chevalier* which is to be part in France and part in Scotland and to deal with Prince Charlie about the year 1749; and now what have I done but begun a third which is to be all moorland

---

1. *David Balfour* was the original title for Stevenson's sequel to *Kidnapped*—a title that was changed to *Catriona* in the UK after serialisation.

together and is to have for a centrepiece a figure that I think you will appreciate—that of the immortal Braxfield. Braxfield himself is my *grand premier*—or since you are so much involved in the British drama, let me say my heavy lead.[2]

Yon was an exquisite story about the barrow, but I think I can beat it. In a little tale of mine, the slashed and gaping ruins of which appeared recently in the *Illustrated London News*, a perfect synod of appalled editors and apologetic friends had sat and wrangled over the thing in private with astonishing results. The flower of their cuts was this. Two little native children were described as wriggling out of their clothes and running away mother-naked. The celestial idiots cut it out.[3] I wish we could afford to do without serial publication altogether. It is odd that

....

2. Stevenson is referring to his new project that would come to be called *Weir of Hermiston* (working title, 'The Justice Clerk'), a novel that remained unfinished at the point of his death in 1894. Stevenson modelled the judge, Adam Weir, Lord Hermiston, on the infamous Lord Braxfield who was influential in suppressing the Friends of the People in the 1790s, sentencing Thomas Muir to fourteen years' transportation.

3. 'Uma; or The Beach of Falesá' was originally published in the *Illustrated London News* through July and August 1892. Stevenson restored a version of this edited line when 'The Beach of Falesá' was included in *Island Nights' Entertainments* (1893). For more on this alteration, see Barry Menikoff, *Robert Louis Stevenson and 'The Beach of Falesá': A Study in Victorian Publishing with the Original Text* (Edinburgh: Edinburgh University Press, 1984), pp. 81–2.

Hardy's adventure with the barrow and mine of the little children should happen in the same year with the publication and success of *Tess*. Surely these editor people are wrong.

Your description of your dealings with Lord Rintoul are frightfully unconscientious. You should never write about anybody until you persuade yourself at least for the moment that you love him: above all anybody on whom your plot revolves. It will always make a hole in the book; and if he have anything to do with the mechanism, prove a stick in your machinery. But you know all this better than I do and it is one of your most promising traits that you do not take your powers too seriously. *The Little Minister* ought to have ended badly; we all know it did; and we are infinitely grateful to you for the grace and good feeling with which you lied about it. If you had told the truth, I for one could never have forgiven you. As you had conceived and written the earlier parts, the truth about the end, though indisputably true to fact, would have been a lie or what is worse a discord in art. If you are going to make a book end badly, it must end badly from the beginning. Now your book began to end well. You let yourself fall in love with, and fondle, and smile at your puppets. Once you had done that your honour was committed—at the cost of

truth to life you were bound to save them. It is
the blot on *Richard Feverel*, for instance, that it
begins to end well; and then tricks you and ends
ill.[4] But in that case, there is worse behind; for
the ill-ending does not inherently issue from the
plot—the story *had*, in fact, *ended well* after the
great last interview between Richard and Lucy—
and the blind, illogical bullet which smashes all
has no more to do between the boards than a fly
has to do with the room into whose open window
it comes buzzing. It might have so happened;
it needed not; and unless needs must, we have
no right to pain our readers. I have had a heavy
case of conscience of the kind about my Braxfield
story. Braxfield—only his name is Hermiston—
has a son who is condemned to death: plainly
there is a fine tempting fitness about this; and I
meant he was to hang. But now on considering
my minor characters, I saw there were five people
who would—in a sense who must—break prison
and attempt his rescue. They were capable hardy
folks too, who might very well succeed. Why
should they not then? Why should not young
Hermiston escape clear out of the country? and
be happy, if he could, with his—but soft! I will
not betray my secret or my heroine. Suffice it

....

4. *The Ordeal of Richard Feverel* (1859) was the first novel written by
George Meredith.

to breathe in your ear that she was what Hardy calls (and others, in their plain way, don't) a Pure Woman.[5] Much virtue in a capital letter—such as yours was.

Write to me again in my infinite distance. Tell me about your new book. No harm in telling *me*; I am too far off to be indiscreet, there are too few near me who would care to hear. I am rushes by the riverside, and the stream is in Babylon; breathe your secrets to me fearlessly; even if the Trade Wind caught and carried them away, there are none to catch them nearer than Australia, unless it were the Tropic Birds. In the unavoidable absence of my Amanuensis,[6] who is buying eels for dinner, I have thus concluded my despatch, like St Paul, with my own hand.[7]

And in the inimitable words of Lord Kames, Faur ye weel, ye Bitch![8]

Yours very truly
Robert Louis Stevenson

---

5. The subtitle of Hardy's *Tess of the D'Urbervilles* was 'A Pure Woman Faithfully Presented'.

6. After suffering from writer's cramp in June 1892, Stevenson dictated many of his letters and works to Isobel Strong, his stepdaughter.

7. 'I, Paul, write this greeting in my own hand' (1 Corinthians 16:21).

8. Before his death, the Scottish judge Lord Kames (1696–1782) is reported to have said to his colleagues: 'Fare ye a' weel, ye bitches!'

6

[*Vailima*]

[Early December 1892]

Dear Mr Barrie,

You will be sick of me soon; I cannot help it.
I have been off my work for some time, and re-
read the *Edinburgh Eleven*, and had a great mind
to write a parody and give you all your sauce back
again, and see how you would like it yourself.[1]
And then I read (for the first time—I know not
how) the *Window in Thrums*; I don't say that it is
better than *The Minister*; it's less of a tale—and
there is a beauty, a material beauty, of the tale
ipse, which clever critics nowadays long and love
to forget;[2] it has more real flaws; but somehow it
is—well, I read it last anyway, and it's by Barrie.
And he's the man for my money. The glove is a
great page; it is startlingly original, and as true as

1. Barrie's book *An Edinburgh Eleven: Pencil Portraits from College Life*
(1889) features a chapter on Stevenson, in which Barrie states that
Stevenson is yet to write his great book.

2. *ipse* is Latin for 'itself'.

death and judgment.[3] Tibbie Birse in the Burial
is great, but I think it was a journalist that got in
the word "official." The same character plainly
had a word to say to Thomas Haggart.[4] Thomas
affects me as a lie—I beg your pardon; doubtless
he was somebody you knew; that leads people so
far astray. The actual is not the true.

I am proud to think you are a Scotchman—
though to be sure I know nothing of that country,
being only an English tourist, quo' Gavin Ogilvy.[5]
I commend the hard case of Mr. Gavin Ogilvy
to J. M. Barrie, whose work is to me a source
of living pleasure and heartfelt national pride.

....

3. 'A Tale of a Glove' is a chapter in Barrie's *A Window in Thrums*, in
which Jess (Jamie's mother) comes to terms with her son having
a girlfriend. In a letter to Henry James, also from December 1892,
Stevenson wrote that it knocked him 'flat' [*The Letters of Robert Louis
Stevenson*, VII, p. 451].

4. In Chapter 7 of *A Window in Thrums*, 'The Statement of Tibbie Birse',
Birse reflects on Pete Lownie's burial. Thomas Haggart is the sarcastic
humourist of Thrums. Referring to *A Window in Thrums* in his letter
to Henry James from December 1892, Stevenson noted of Barrie: 'Stuff
in that young man; but he must see and not be too funny. Genius in
him, but there's a journalist at his elbow—there's the risk' [*The Letters
of Robert Louis Stevenson*, VII, p. 451].

5. In *An Edinburgh Eleven* (written under Barrie's pseudonym, Gavin
Ogilvy), Barrie critiques Stevenson for offering superficial portrayals
of Scots and Scotland in his writing. Commenting on Alan Breck
Stewart, one of the protagonists in Stevenson's *Kidnapped*, Barrie wrote
that 'an artistic Englishman or American could have done it. Scottish
religion, I think, Mr. Stevenson has never understood, except as the
outsider misunderstands it' (p. 107).

There are two of us now that the Shirra might have patted on the head.[6] And please do not think, when I thus seem to bracket myself with you, that I am wholly blinded with vanity. Jess is beyond my frontier line; I could not touch her skirt; I have no such glamour of twilight on my pen. I am a capable artist; but it begins to look to me as if you were a man of genius. Take care of yourself for my sake. It's a devilish hard thing for a man who writes so many novels as I do, that I should get so few to read. And I can read yours, and I love them.

A pity for you that my amanuensis is not on stock to-day, and my own hand perceptibly worse than usual.

Yours,
Robert Louis Stevenson

December 5th, 1892

PS. We have, for a wonder of wonder, visitors here. They are a mother and daughter by the name of Fraser.[7] They seem to know you, and I

6. Walter Scott became Sheriff Depute, or Shirra, of Selkirkshire in 1799.

7. Marie Fraser played Lady Yuill in the Criterion performance of Barrie and Marriott Watson's play *Richard Savage* in April 1891. She

must say I feel as if I rather knew you myself since
the daughter acted you for my entertainment
one afternoon. This is put in malice prepense
in the hopes of stirring you up to be lively on
the subject of the Frasers. And anyway you will
have the fun of seeing her act me before you are
very much older. They tell me your health is not
strong. Man, come out here and try the Prophet's
chamber.[8] The whole family smoke, and that all
day long, except when they are suffering from
the practice and have sworn off. But reassure
yourself, these revivals never last long. There's
only one bad point to us—we do rise early.
The Amanuensis states that you are a lover of
silence—and that ours is a noisy house—and she
is a chatter-box—I am not answerable for these
statements, though I do think there is a touch of
garrulity about my premises. We have so little
to talk about, you see. The house is three miles
from town in the midst of great silent forests.
There is a burn close by, and when we are not
talking you can hear the burn, and the birds, and
the sea breaking on the coast three miles away
and six hundred feet below us, and about three
times a month a bell—I don't know where the

visited Samoa in 1892 with her mother and went on to publish an
account of her time there, titled *In Stevenson's Samoa* (1895).

8. A site of respite. The phrase derives from the biblical tale of the prophet
Elisha, who was offered shelter by a Shunammite woman (2 Kings 4:10).

bell is nor who rings it, it may be the bell in Hans
Andersen's story for all I know.[9] It is never hot
here—86 in the shade is about our hottest—and
it is never cold except just in the early mornings.
Take it for all in all, I suppose this island climate
to be by far the healthiest in the world—even
the influenza entirely lost its sting. Only two
patients died and one was a man nearly eighty
and the other a child below four months. I
won't tell you if it is beautiful, for I want you
to come and see for yourself. Everybody on the
premises except my wife has some Scotch blood
in their veins—I beg your pardon—except the
natives—and then my wife is a Dutchwoman—
and the natives are the next thing conceivable to
Highlanders before the forty-five.[10] We would
have some grand cracks!

R. L. S.
Come, it will broaden your mind, and be the
making of me.

....

9. In Hans Christian Andersen's 'The Bell' (1845), the people of a large
town try to locate the invisible, holy bell that rings in the forest.

10. 'The forty-five' is a reference to the 1745 Jacobite Rising, which
ended with the Battle of Culloden in 1746. Stevenson compared
Highlanders to native Samoans in several writings; see Roslyn Jolly,
'Stevenson and the Pacific', in *The Edinburgh Companion to Robert Louis
Stevenson*, ed. by Penny Fielding (Edinburgh: Edinburgh University
Press, 2010), pp. 118–33.

7

Garrick Club
W.C.

December 24, 1892

Dear Mr Stevenson,

I am celebrating Christmas Eve by writing to you. Whether it is also Boxing Night I don't know, but I fear you do as you can speak calmly of having eels for dinner, while we are freezing. I picture you in a suit of bananas (I feel that this is not quite the word) enticing the monkeys to fling cocoanuts at you, which is my notion of life in Samoa. I once wrote a newspaper article on Christmas—about a man who said he murdered two or three Waits (he could never remember the exact number) and buried them in the quadrangle of his university.[1] My doctor was reading it the next time I saw him and he said, "Have you seen this horrible affair—most cold-blooded murder I ever read of." At first I

---

1. Waits are singers who perform on the streets around Christmas. Barrie is referencing a story that would become Chapter 30, 'The Murder in the Inn,' of his book *My Lady Nicotine* (1890). This chapter focuses on a bachelor who has to choose between smoking and his wife-to-be.

thought of explaining, then I weakly agreed with him, which shows you the kind of man I am. Another article about a man, name of Robbins, who committed suicide rather than write any more Jubilee articles was taken seriously by the London correspondent of an Australian paper, who wrote, "One of the saddest affairs in connection with the Jubilee is the tragic death of Mr. Robbins, a much respected journalist who" etc. Another about a dog I said I had found (when its owner was looking the other way) led to my having a charming correspondence with a lady who had lost a dog and felt sure that this was the one. My society for providing a room in the Strand into which poets could rush when the afflatus was on them drew three letters wanting the society's address.[2] Another society provided reminiscences for biographers who had run short, and a correspondent wanted a dozen or two for a book on German emperors.

I think the first four chapters of "David Balfour" the finest beginning you have ever done. The opening paragraph is wonderfully vivid. I have a theory that all first sentences are ungrammatical (owing to the care that is taken

2. The Strand is a major thoroughfare near the Thames in London, known for printing and publishing. *The Strand Magazine*, which published the Sherlock Holmes stories, was established there in 1891.

with them). Can't prove *as yet* that yours is so in
this instance. Must have another go at it.

In that letter I had from you eight years ago
you said that you were planning a story of the
Great High Road.[3] Where is it? It delights me
that all your projects are so Scotch. "The Young
Chevalier" is a fine title. (So was "Harry Shovel."
Where is he?)[4] Is not the pursuit of names an
exhilarating sport? I know a man called Wolf
Flanagan, and that is why I like him. I feel that
he is the villain of an unwritten book, and that
you are the writer thereof. I expect you won't
be able to resist this. It is my Xmas gift to you.
He could play second lead to Braxfield. Why
shouldn't I write a little bit of the book myself
(you go and eat eels)?—"As the prisoner was
ushered into the court house, Braxfield was
seen to turn pale. All men wondered. Was it a
sudden illness? Was it a presentiment? Twice
Braxfield rose to ask the prisoner's name—twice
he swallowed his unspoken words. A strange

---

3. The whereabouts of this letter is unknown.

4. In his essay on Stevenson in *An Edinburgh Eleven*, Barrie relates that
Stevenson is working on a novel titled 'Harry Shovel: A Romance of
the Peninsular War'. Stevenson's novel *Adventures of Henry Shovel*
(which he also referred to as 'The Shovels of Newton French') was left
unfinished at his death. The first three chapters were subsequently
published in 1923, in volume 25 of the Vailima edition of *The Works of
Robert Louis Stevenson*.

stillness fell upon the court house. At last
Braxfield, speaking with an emotion that
was foreign to the man, demanded harshly,
'Prisoner, your name?' The prisoner folded his
arms, and with the modesty of one who knows
that his triumph has come, replied calmly
'Wolf Flanagan.' Braxfield shuddered and sank
cowering into his chair. *He knew that in that name
he had met his match.*"

Again, where is your Queen Mary story? You
need not say that you never contemplated one.
Your nationality forbids—even though you do
eat eels. (It is a remarkable thing, but I feel as if
I had eaten those eels). I have thought over my
Queen Mary story, but to get away from it for
the present rather than to write it. It opens in
Edinburgh of today with the birth of a draper's
son who comes into the world with a tendency
to hide one of his fingers. Mary did this, and
we plod back through his ancestors to discover
how, ending with the Kirk of Field.[5] "Queen
Mary's Ring" is all that is written of it as yet.[6]

5. Kirk o' Field in Edinburgh is best known as the site of the murder of
Lord Darnley, the husband of Mary Queen of Scots.

6. At Jedburgh in 1928, as part of a benefit to raise funds to maintain
a house once occupied by Mary Queen of Scots, Barrie made a speech
where he told the audience that Mary Stuart had returned to Jedburgh
the previous night, and told him that the casket letters were not genuine.
His speech is reproduced in *M'Connachie and J. M. B.*, pp. 139–45.

The story that will probably be my next is just begun, called "Sentimental Tommy," an attempt at drawing a real man of learning after he has ceased to admire his subject.[7] What you say about one's not being entitled to write of anybody till we love him pleases me much. I feel that this book is bound to be a melancholy failure unless I love poor Tommy all the time (and probably whether or no). We have had a little tiff at the start because Thomas wanted to put Thrums into the first sentence, while my grand ambition is to dodge the place altogether. I have gone through the first chapter and pencilled out the Thrums, much as I used to weed a carrot bed. At present we have compromised, he undertaking to lay the scene elsewhere if I let him write from Thrums. I foresee complications, and the dominie will be a bit sulky. Then "Haggart the Humourist" is half written, but I say that a time came when he discovered that he had never been a humourist, which he denies, so he is shelved until he can listen to reason.

Now you know more of my projects than any other. I had a play produced in New York lately and have one in London and have finished an

....

7. Barrie spent several years working on his novel *Sentimental Tommy,* which was published in 1896.

opera,[8] but the drama is abandoned for books for a long time now.

I get most of my news about London from a man in India, so anything I could tell you would probably be stale. They are still discussing style at the Savile.[9] Somebody has discovered that St. Andrews is called after Andrew Lang.[10] I have promised Grant Allen's wife not to call him "The Man who is not allowed" any more, because it keeps her awake at nights.[11] There is a rumour that a member has spoken to another member in the Athenaeum.[12] Ibsen is to be brought over and

....

8. In 1892, Barrie's play *Walker, London* was staged in London and his latest play, *The Professor's Love Story*, was performed in New York. His opera *Jane Annie*, a collaboration with Arthur Conan Doyle, proved to be a flop.

9. The Savile Club was established in 1868 by a group of prominent writers and artists. Both Barrie and Stevenson became members.

10. Scottish author, folklorist and psychical researcher, Andrew Lang, had a sustained correspondence with Stevenson; his letters are published in the book *Dear Stevenson* (1990), edited by Marysa Demoor. Barrie wasn't as close to Lang but he did publish a satirical article in *The Scots Observer*, titled 'Mr. Plagiary Lang', under the pseudonym 'A Woman of Letters'. The article mocked those who failed to recognise the fact that Lang's book *Old Friends* (1890) was a series of parodies [Beinecke Library GEN MSS 1400, Series II, box 50, folder 1052].

11. In 1895, Allen would write a controversial 'new woman' novel, *The Woman Who Did*, which was criticised by both conservatives and feminists.

12. The Athenæum Club was founded in 1824. Stevenson was a member and Barrie became one in 1902; his proposed membership was seconded by Lord Rosebery [Chaney, p. 191].

made poet laureate. We are presenting Besant
with an ink bottle (!) for being chairman of the
Authors Society or something. Any corks in
Samoa? Am told Hardy's new novel now in serial
is about a man who falls in love first with one
woman, then twenty years afterwards with her
daughter, then twenty years afterwards with the
granddaughter, whom he marries. I put my hand
on his shoulder the other night, and he started,
as if he thought it was the policeman at last.[13] I
wish you would send me a picture of your house
at Samoa. It would make me feel a 1000 miles
nearer you.

Yours ever,
J. M. *Barrie*

13. Barrie and Hardy remained friends until Hardy's death in 1928.
In September 1931, Barrie gave a speech at the unveiling of a statue of
Hardy in Dorchester, which is reproduced in *M'Connachie and J. M. B.*,
pp. 219–22. Stevenson first met Hardy in Dorchester in 1885, and he
even proposed dramatising Hardy's *The Mayor of Casterbridge*, which
Hardy assented to [Thomas Hardy, 'Robert Louis Stevenson', in *I Can
Remember Robert Louis Stevenson*, ed. by Rosaline Masson (Edinburgh:
W. & R. Chambers, 1925), pp. 214–16].

8

Garrick Club
W.C.

29 January 1893

Dear R. L. S,

You must let me say at the start that I have an
affection for the man who wears these initials. I
might not have let on in ordinary circumstances,
but on Saturday night I was shaken out of all
reserve by a telegram from San Francisco in the
evening papers that you were very ill. I could
not do any work. I cabled to America to discover
how the story arose. In the meantime those
who knew better how to get at the facts had a
cablegram from Auckland that you are all right.
It is good news to many and to me. Anstey
and I had a dinner over it. To be blunt I have
discovered (have suspected it for some time) that
I love you, and if you had been a woman—

Your last letter was about the most generous
any man ever wrote to another, but it leaves
me still with sufficient sense to continue to sit
at your feet, instead of standing beside you on

my tiptoes. I await Miss Fraser's imitations of
you with impatience. When she played in my
dramar [sic] I never was quite sure whether she
was alive. I conducted affairs then on strictly
unbusinesslike principles, and doubled my
villain's salary *because he was so bad*. He mouthed
and strided at rehearsals so that I gloried in
him though I knew he would kill the play. To
rectify the impressions of me Miss Fraser
has left behind at Samoa I don't see why I
shouldn't draw myself.

(1) <u>Appearance</u>: The face is all right, except
for a suggestion of weakness in the mouth.
Moustachios considerable, but one usually
longer than the other, owing to ceaseless
attempts with scissors to bring them into
harmony. When at a mixed school, the girls
took a plebiscite about which boy had most
engaging smile. Got highest marks. Have
not smiled since. Can't. Figure mean. What
there is of it, fair. Not enough of it.

(2) <u>Manners</u>. None. When taking a lady in to
dinner (seldom do it) unblushingly say to her,
quoting from well-known writer, "Don't you
think the old plan better, when the gentleman
took the lady's hand?" Being indistinct of

speech (and usually regretting remark when in middle of it) is not often heard. She begs pardon, by which time dining room is reached. Lately desperate lady at dinner said to him, "Didn't catch your name." He said wasn't surprised (never catch hers). She continued, "And don't know what you do." He said, "No, suppose not." The end.

<u>J. L. Toole to Henry Irving</u>[1] (Hats off) A gentle creature. Just looks at you when you say anything funny. Like him best when he goes away.

<u>In the opinion of the ladies </u>(which after all is the main thing). Is that Mr. Barrie? Well, I am. <u>In the opinion of Himself.</u> An absorbing study. As for the hostesses, they say, "He is quite worth asking once." And this is the character you would rashly invite to Samoa.

Act 1

<u>R.L.S.</u> Yes, he has arrived. I have put him into a

---

1. John Lawrence Toole and Henry Irving were famous Victorian actors and theatrical producers. Toole directed Barrie's *Walker, London* (1892) and he starred in *Ibsen's Ghost*, both of which played at Toole's Theatre. Henry Irving became aware of Barrie when the morality of his first play, *Bandelero the Bandit*—written as a schoolboy for his Dumfries theatre club, was questioned by a local minister. In response, Irving became a patron of the club.

bedroom. I advised him to rest for a bit—for as long as he could.

Mrs. R.L.S. What did he say?

R.L.S. He said "H'm." He has been saying that all the way up from the boat.

Mrs. R.L.S. How did he strike you on the whole?

R.L.S (glumly) Perhaps he will improve after he has rested a bit. I told him he would have to be tattooed before dinner.

Mrs. R.L.S. What did he say?

R.L.S. H'm.

Act 2

R.L.S. Well, what do you think of him?

Mrs R.L.S. (goodnaturedly) Perhaps he isn't very well.

R.L.S. But what did he say to you?

Mrs. R.L.S. It was rather strange for a first remark.

R.L.S. I bet you eels for dinner that he said "H'm."

Mrs R.L.S. No.

R.L.S. He didn't? Come, come, he improves.

Mrs. R.L.S. He stammered, and then asked earnestly if I didn't think the old way of entering a dining room holding the lady's hand—

Act 3 In the kitchen.

Cook Peloo pah peloo (native interjection) And
    did his face light up whatever when he saw
    the plum pudding all ablazing?

Maid Peloo, pah peloo. No, he asked if he could
    light his pipe at it.

Between the Acts

Mrs. R.L.S. Why are you tearing so many pages
    out of the calendar?

R.L.S. H'm.

Mrs. R.L.S. He has taught you that habit!

R.L.S I mean I am tearing them out because I
    feel that it must be months since he came.

Act 4

At last he is on board the departing vessel.

Mrs. R.L.S. Poor girl.

R.L.S. (sarcastically) That is the captain. Ask
    him if he doesn't think the old plan of taking
    the lady's hand—

Mrs. R.L.S. Poor girl.

R.L.S.   Tell them all in London that I am h'm.

Mrs. R.L.S. (weeping) Poor girl.

R.L.S. Now that the gangway is between us I feel
    as if we could be friends again.

Mrs. R.L.S. Poor girl (hysterically). (Exit boat)

R.L.S. What girl are you talking about?

<u>Mrs. R.L.S.</u> It had suddenly struck me, what if he
were to marry!

That is a photograph that some people would
recognise—including perhaps Miss Fraser.
(You observe that all the time I am consumed
with curiosity to know what she made of me).
However it would only be a true one if you were
they, and though it were gospel I would, if other
things did not come in the way, start for Samoa
by the first train to Victoria from here (and they
run every ten minutes). That time I honestly
do believe would suffice for the packing of all
my belongings, which consist when I come to
think of it, of my mother's photograph. And
there is the real reason why I don't start off for
Samoa and settle in it and have such times with
you as I feel I can never have with any other
man and reveal to you (insist on it) the real JMB
who has been so far carefully concealed from
his "intimate friends." The fact is that I have
a passion for my mother and my young sister
which makes me stay at home. People often ask
why I don't travel, and I never tell them the real
reason, but there it is. My mother and father
live at Kirriemuir (just opposite the Window in
Thrums) and I am always with them except for

some months when I am here when my sister comes with me. My sister was to be married to a Free Kirk minister, my greatest friend, last June, and on the 8th of May he was flung from his horse and killed. I shall never forget that I wrote to you on the 8th May and that the telegram which made me begin the world again arrived before the letter was posted.

Such a home life as yours seems to me an ideal one for a literary man—far removed from the trivialities of club life, and with all those around you whom you most care for. One of the grandest lies in the world of letters (which is as big as Ailsa Craig)[2] is that one must "come up to town occasionally, otherwise he loses touch," God knows what of. One thing sure is that you don't lose touch in "David Balfour." I have just finished part three and still it is by far your best. There is no doubt about it at all. You have never got near anything so good as David himself. I rose from the scene by the wayside between him and Catriona feeling that they were two of the bravest, most innocent and pathetic figures in all fiction. And again that feeling came back when I read of David's fight that was no fight, with Duncansby. I see that Alan Breck is coming

2. The Ailsa Craig is an island off the coast of Ayrshire in Scotland.

on, and I tremble for him for I believe David will dwarf him. I used to think Ollala (is that the proper arrangement of the dratted ls?) your best girl,[3] but she is to Catriona as my pencil => (that is it, life size) to an elvint.

(That is the beginning of an elvint).[4]

Let me say it is pretty rough on me your getting hold of the "Edinburgh Eleven." I was a boy then. As for Haggart you are quite right but see if I don't make him human yet, and dedicate the work to you.

Latest from Thrums. Weaver brought up for hitting another man. The defence, "My Lord, I thocht he would hae joukit."

Also at a funeral. To guest, "You'll find the whisky on the dresser. My father's on the table."

Yours ever,
J. M. Barrie

P.S. I am coming someday.

3. 'Olalla' is a Gothic short story, which originally appeared in *The Court and Society Review* (1885), before being included in *The Merry Men and Other Tales and Fables* (1887).

4. An elvint, or elvand, is a Scots word for a measuring rod.

doubt about it at all. You have never got near anything so good as David himself. I rose from the scene of the wonder'd between him & Catriona feeling that they were two of the bravest most innocent & pathetic figures in all fiction. And again that feeling came back when I read of David's fight that was no fight, with Duncansby, I see that Alan Breck is coming on, I humble for him for I believe David will dwarf him. I asked L think Ollalla (is that the the proper arrangement of the drawtled £s?) your best girl, but she is L Catriona as my pencil

☐ (that is it, life size) to an elvint-

(That is the beginning of an elvint.

Let me say it is pretty rough on me your getting hold of the Edinburgh Eleven. I was a boy then. As for Haggaalty on an great night, but see i' I don't make him human yet and dedicate this work to you.
Latest from Thrums. Weaver brought up for hitting another man. The defence, My Lord, I thought he wd have jooked. Also at a funeral. To guest, You'll find the whisky on the dresser. My father's on this table.

P.S I am coming someday.

Yours ever
J. M. Barrie

3958

9

Vailima, Samoa

April 2nd or 3rd 1893

My dear Barrie,

Tit for tat. Here follows a catalogue of
my menagerie:

R. L. S.
The Tame Celebrity.
Native name, *Tusi tala.*[1]

Exceedingly lean, dark, rather ruddy—black
eyes **(drawing book eyes—*Amanuensis*)**[2]
crow's-footed, beginning to be grizzled, general
appearance of a blasted boy—or blighted youth—
or to borrow Carlyle on De Quincey "Child that
has been in hell." Past eccentric—obscure and
oh no we never mention it—Present industrious

---

1. Tusitala—'teller of tales'—was Stevenson's local name in Samoa.
Bold type is used in Letters 9 and 10 to indicate the use of red ink in
the manuscripts.

2. Throughout this letter, Stevenson's amanuensis and stepdaughter,
Isobel Strong, makes interjections that appear in brackets in red ink.
At the top of the letter, Strong includes an illustration (also in red ink)
of Stevenson lying in bed reading the 'Complete Works' of 'J. M. Barrie'.

respectable and fatuously contented. Used to
be very fond of talking about art, don't talk
about it any more. Is restrained by his family
from talking about Origin of Polynesian Race.
Really knows a good deal but has lived so long
with aforesaid family and foremast hands, that
you might talk a week to him and never guess it.
(**This is the grossest injustice—what that man
knows about** *chiffons* **is something wonderful,
and he never tires of it.** *Am.***)** Friendly grocer
in Sydney: "It has been a most agreeable surprise
to meet you Mr. Stevenson. I would never have
guessed you were a literary man." Name in
family, The Tame Celebrity. Cigarettes without
intermission except when coughing or kissing.
Hopelessly entangled in apron strings. Drinks
plenty. Curses some. Temper unstable. Manners
purple on an emergency, but liable to trances.
Essentially the common old copy-book gentleman
of commerce: if accused of cheating at cards,
would feel bound to blow out's brains, little as he
would like the job. Has been an invalid for ten
years, but can boldly claim that you can't tell it
on him. (**When he's well he looks like a brown
boy with an uncertain temper, but when he
is ill he's a rose-garden invalid with a sainted
smile.** *Am.***)** Given to explaining the universe.
Scotch, sir, Scotch.

Fanny V. de G. Stevenson.[3]
The Weird Woman.
Native name, *Tamaitai*.

That is what you will have to look out for,
Mr Barrie. If you don't get on with her, it's a pity
about your visit. She runs the show. Infinitely
little, extraordinary wig of gray curls,[4] handsome
waxen face like Napoleon's, insane black eyes,
boy's hands, tiny bare feet, a cigarette, wild blue
native dress usually spotted with garden mould.
In company manners presents the appearance
of a little timid and precise old maid of the days
of prunes and prism; you look for the reticule.[5]
**(But wouldn't be surprised to find a dagger
in her garter, *Am*.)** Hellish energy; relieved
by fortnights of entire hibernation. Can make
anything from a house to a row, all fine and
large of their kind. My uncle, after seeing her
for the first time: "Yes Louis, you have done
well. I married a bizzom myself and have never
regretted it." Mrs. Fraser (*et pour cause*): "She has
the indomitable will of Richelieu." **(Reminds**

3. Stevenson married Fanny Van de Grift Osbourne in 1880 in San
Francisco. They had met in the latter half of the 1870s in Grez-sur-
Loing, France when Fanny was still married to Samuel Osbourne.

4. I have retained Isobel Strong's American spelling of 'grey' here.

5. A draw-string handbag.

me of Madam Esmond in *The Virginians*. A.)[6]
Doctors everybody, will doctor you, cannot
be doctored herself. The Living Partizan: a
violent friend, a brimstone enemy. Imaginary
conversation after your visit: "I like Mr. Barrie. I
don't like anybody else. I don't like anybody that
don't like him. When he took me in to dinner
he made the wittiest remark I ever heard. 'Don't
you think' he said 'the old fashioned way— etc.'"
Is always either loathed or slavishly adored;
indifference impossible. The natives think her
uncanny and that devils serve her. Dreams
dreams, and sees visions.

Isobel Stewart Strong.[7]
Your humble servant the Amanuensis.
Native Name, *Teuila*.
Believed on the beach to be my illegitimate
daughter by a Morocco woman. When we
wish to please her we say she is slender. Rich
dark colour; taken in Sydney for an islander.

6. Cardinal Richelieu was a French clergyman and statesman in the
seventeenth century, known for his authoritarianism and developing
the centralised state. Madam Esmond is a confrontational, scornful
figure in William Makepeace Thackeray's *The Virginians* (1857–59).

7. Isobel (or 'Belle') Strong, Fanny's daughter, was born in 1858 and
regularly served as Stevenson's amanuensis from 1892. In that year, she
divorced her husband, Joseph Dwight Strong; their son, Austin Strong,
lived with her and the Stevensons at Vailima.

Eyes enormous and particoloured, one and three-fifths brown the other two-fifths golden.[8]

> Her long dark hair deep as her knees
> And thrid with the living silver sees—[9]

unpublished poem—ahem! Has made a hussar blush: fact.[10] Doesn't go in for intellect—still less for culture—**(Unfair! "Life is a positive mixture of heterogeneous changes both simultaneous and successive in co-respondence to external sequences and co-existences." Written from memory. How is that for intellect? *Am.*)** When a cultured person, trying to establish relations with her, asked if over-education were not the curse of the present century, she replied "Yes. I feel it myself. When I lie awake nights and think how much I know it makes me tired." Reads nothing but novels; likes these good eg. *Little Minister* and *The Pariah*; couldn't read *Tess*. With her spelling you are already acquainted; my prices are coming down since I began to employ her. Caricatures cleverly. Thing she likes best in

---

8. The word 'she' appears after this sentence in the manuscript in a different colour of ink. It may be the beginning of an abandoned sentence.

9. This is an excerpt from Stevenson's poem 'Mother and Daughter', which was published as part of *The Vailima Edition of the Works of Robert Louis Stevenson* in 1922.

10. A hussar is a member of a class of light cavalry.

the world, dress for herself and others—rather
adornment. Will arrange your hair and stick
flowers about you till you curse. Meaning of her
native name, The Adorner of the Ugly. Even a
stiff six feet two English guest learned to kneel
daily for his wreath, and the native boys go to her
to have their ties put on. Runs me like a baby in a
perambulator, sees I'm properly dressed, bought
me silk socks and made me wear them, takes care
of me when I am sick, and I don't know what the
devil she doesn't do for me when I'm well, from
writing my books to trimming my nails. **(I tried
once to shave him too, but that alas was a
failure. *Am*)** Has a growing conviction that she
is the author of my works. Manages the house
and the house boys who are very fond of her. An
unaffected Pagan, and worships an idol with lights
and flowers. Does all the haircutting of the family.
Will cut yours, and doubtless object to the way
you part it. Mine has been re-organised twice.

Lloyd Osbourne.[11]
The Boy.
Native name, *Loia*.

Six foot. Blond. Eyeglasses. British eyeglasses
too. Address varying from an elaborate civility

11. Born in 1868, Samuel Lloyd Osbourne, Fanny's son, co-authored three
books with Stevenson: *The Wrong Box*, *The Ebb-Tide* and *The Wrecker*.

to a freezing haughtiness. Decidedly witty. Astonishingly ignorant—the original young man whose education was neglected, and it was I who neglected it—yet somehow you would almost never find it out **(I never have.** *Am.***)** Has seen an enormous amount of the world for his age. Keeps nothing of youth but some of its intolerance. Unexpected soft streak for the forlorn. When he is good he is very very good, but when he is cross he is horrid. Of Dutch ancestry, and has spells known in the family as "Cold blasts from Holland." Exacting with the boys, and yet they like him. Rather stiff with his equals, but apt to be very kindly with his inferiors. The only undemonstrative member of the family, which otherwise wears its heart upon both sleeves; and except for my purple patches, the only mannered one. Has tried to learn fifteen instruments; has learned none but is willing to try another tomorrow. *Signe particulier:*[12] when he thrums or tootles on any of these instruments, or even turns a barrel-organ, he insists on public and sustained applause, and the strange thing is he doesn't seem to demand any for his stories. This trait is supposed to be unique. He is his mother's curly headed boy.

12. Distinguishing mark.

Family Life

The Boy, the Amanuensis and the Tame Celebrity
all play on instruments, and all ill. But you
need not applaud the two last, little they'll
reck if you'll let them play on. Conversation,
surprisingly free; at times embarrassingly so
when guests are present. General character
of life: a solid comfortable selfishness—guests
preferred to be selfish also. N.B. No attention
paid to guests. Clothing, you may find Loia in
pajamas of which he has lost the string, soaked
through and bedaubed with mud; or you may
find him in white coat tie and shirt, gaudyish
sash, and excruciatingly elegant riding breeches
and boots; to say nothing of silver mounted
riding whip and sapphire studs.[13] Take me at the
present moment, and my costume consists of one
flannel undershirt and one pair of striped pajama
trousers all told—I beg your pardon, I forgot two
rings and one cigarette, but you see the process
is exhaustive. On the other hand you might find
me in cords and fancy boots, with a velvet jacket
chosen by the Amanuensis to the exact shade of
harmony. My wife's usual dress will scarcely bear

13. On the left-hand side of the manuscript letter are four sketches by
Isobel Strong (in red ink), of the family members and their differing
clothing styles.

to be dwelt upon; but sir, when you told her the old-fashioned way etc., she was in black velvet and duchesse lace, and I will trouble you for how she looked. The career of the Amanuensis would require a pen more accomplished than mine. Her effects are various, sometimes gaudy. Now she is to be seen in bare feet with toe-rings, and anon she is troubling the world with silk stockings, and these are sometimes blue. *Absit omen.*[14] Her frocks and my wife's are all (to do the creatures justice) on the same pattern, the native pattern, and fully more like chemises. But the Amanuensis calls in turn into the field every colour known under heaven; she goes through similar changing phases with her hair of which there is so much that the combinations and permutations are practically inexhaustible; and after each fresh make-up she appears among us for approval and weeps if it be withheld. **(There are different ways of withholding approval. One way "You look much prettier with your hair dressed low." Another "With your hair on top you look like a moon faced idiot with water on the brain." It is then I cry—and so would you. Am.)** Thus we go up, up, up, and thus we go down, down, down.

14. May omen be absent (in other words, may what is said not come true).

And you can see for yourself it is a somewhat dressy spot though not at all like Piccadilly.

Another thing you must be prepared for—and that is the arrival of strange old shell-back guests out of every quarter of the island world, their mouths full of oaths for which they will punctiliously apologise, their clothes unmistakably purchased in a trade room, each probably followed by a dusky bride. These you are to expect to see hailed with acclamations, and dragged in as though they were dukes and duchesses. **(But do you drag in dukes and duchesses? Am.)** For though we may be out of touch with "God knows what", we are determined to keep in touch with Apemama and the Marquesas.[15]

Miss Fraser gave a really neat and convincing representation of J.M.B. sitting in a large chair and saying *h'm*. It was the only clever thing I ever saw her do or could ever suppose her doing. **(To me she described you enthusiastically but somewhat vaguely as "a dear!"' Am.)** Your doubts as to her vitality were probably grounded. She is the only actor I ever knew who did not care even to talk about the stage.

....

15. Apemama (or Abemama) is an atoll in the Gilbert Islands. The Marquesas Islands lie 3,500km east of Samoa. Stevenson wrote about both locations in *In the South Seas* (1896).

By the bye a passage in the above has nearly blown up this family. It was faithfully submitted to all concerned and admitted to be on the whole a faithful and unvarnished account; but after a series of painful discussions we have decided to recall the word "selfishness." Loia prefers the phrase "a *Wuthering Heights* impatience." You may take it at that.

And now my dear fellow I want to thank you very heartily for your last letter. That you should have telegraphed to the States, and that you and Anstey should have dined together in honour of the better news, has infinitely touched me. I am quite sure that I know you and quite sure that you know me. People mayn't be like their books, they *are* their books. All that we want to do now is to meet—again. Do try and bring this visit about before anything happens; and to show that my eccentric family are at one with me in the invitation here follow the signatures of all

Fanny V. de G. Stevenson
Isobel Strong
Lloyd Osbourne
Robert Louis Stevenson

Stevenson sent several pictures to Barrie with Letter 9;
this portrait, inscribed to him, was most likely one of them.
From I Can Remember Robert Louis Stevenson,
ed. by Rosaline Masson (Edinburgh: W. & R. Chambers, 1922).

10

Kirriemuir
N.B.

23 July 1893

My dear Tusi Tala,

Greeting. I was expecting from the post only
business letters when in he walks instead with
your pictures. And I have not had such a joyous
disappointment since my boyhood, when I
once lost a penny at a market (I used to hold
the horses, just like *Shakespeare*)[1] and going forth
to search the world for it found eightpence!
That was a day. So I tell you is this. You are
all three on the mantelpiece already between
Meredith's house and his chalet, so that we are
a regular picnic somewhere about the long apple
tree at Box Hill and divided into two parties
by the clock. I have put two and two together
pretty smartly, namely the photographs and
your inventory of your household, and beg
to announce with a good deal of elation that

1. Barrie refers to the myth that Shakespeare started his theatrical
career by holding horses for theatre-goers.

Tamaitai is in my opinion the kind I can get
round and Teuila the kind that gets round me.[2]
It is Tamaitai's eyes that give her away. I read
in them an extraordinary tolerance for boys,
and I am a boy though I keep it dark. When the
blinds are down I jump over chairs and play wild
pranks, and my word of honour I feel I could
carry on in this way before Tamaitai, and she
understand that there was no ill in me so long
as she was there to manage me. I guess Tamaitai
was brought into the world to take care of daft
literary characters, with just this one weakness,
that in moments of impulse she can be got to
join them and then don't we just have a gorgeous
holiday, and which is leader, I should like to
know! But next morning Tamaitai does not
know what you mean if you refer to yestreen,
and if I had an amanuensis in red ink I could
draw you Tamaitai now possessed of domesticity,[3]
a terrible figure on a table all of a quiver because
she cannot knock nails into four walls at one
blow (observe in the distance Tusi Tala and Loia
flying toward the shore) and doing sixhanded
things till she sinks exhausted but happy on

2. 'To get round'—to get your own way through flattery.

3. In the previous letter, Isobel Strong's interjections were written in red
ink. Her illustrations are also sketched using red ink.

the couch. (Observe Tusi Tala sauntering back with a cigarette and pointing out to her that she has been overdoing it). I didn't need to be told that Tamaitai was "infinitely little." The more you like them the less they get. My Babbie was biggish in the first chapters but as I warmed to her she got so small that the editor of "Good Words" complained, saying that he had accepted her as a "braw kimmer" and soon you would need a candle to look for her. I also enlarged her mouth at his request. My native Samoan name is Softy Softy, which means the Good-Natured Author.

Nothing would flatter me so much as having my hair cut by Teuila, and I wouldn't cry out though we seemed to spill something like red ink. The barbers always say "Hair cut?" to me though they cut it yesterday, and I have a horrid fear that one of them will get round me some day and make me take the oil. As for reorganising my hair, I have felt for years that there is a great chance there for somebody.

You can tell Loia that a most mysterious affair has occurred, nothing short of this that when the packet arrived his photograph was no longer in it. As I cannot think so badly of him or believe that it never was there I conclude that

it was stealthily removed at the post office here where we have a young lady who had probably opened the inventory and been enamoured of the sketch of Loia in red ink. If there is any truth in a report I heard at Cambridge that Loia is coming to the old country (wouldn't if I were he) he is hereby elected an Allahakbarrie.[4] The fame of the Allahakbarries has probably reached Samoa, it being nothing less than a cricket club of which I am captain, and the name as near as we can get at it means "Heaven help the Barries." We are all literary hands, and among the honorary patrons is Alan Breck, Esq. Extract from the club card—

Barrie (Capt.) An ideal captain. A treat to see
    him tossing the penny. Once took a wicket.
    Takes all the credit when one of his side
    makes a run.
Marriot Watson[5] (Pomaded! Oh Tusi Tala!)
    A capital man in the train going down.
    Safe bat in the train. Loses confidence when
    told to go in.

4. The Allahakbarries was the affectionate name for Barrie's amateur cricket team, which was set up in 1890. Several famous writers played for the team, including A. A. Milne, Arthur Conan Doyle, P. G. Wodehouse and G. K. Chesterton.

5. Henry Brereton Marriot Watson was an Australian-born novelist. He co-wrote the play *Richard Savage* (1891) with Barrie.

Conan Doyle Hits blooming hard, blooming
high and blooming seldom.

Harold Frederic[6] Safe scorer on a ground that
suits him. Has not yet found a ground to suit
him.

Bernard Partridge[7] The Demon bowler. Breaks
everything except the ball. Smashes his own
side. Will bowl at the wicket and nail square
leg in the stomach.

F. Anstey[8] Stays in London and cheers at two,
four and six o'clock. &c, &c.

We have already played a team of elderly
Surrey rustics, and having filled them first with
ale won a glorious victory, marred by Frederic
who was always photographing the ball when
he should have been catching it. Doyle defied
the best bowling of Shere (but not until he was
out),[9] Watson made one in masterly manner and
Partridge played a dashing innings for nothing.
The way I ordered my team to stop smoking

6. Harold Frederic was an American journalist and novelist who
became friends with Barrie.

7. Bernard Partridge was an English illustrator, who would go on to
illustrate Barrie's novel *Tommy and Grizel* (1900).

8. F. Anstey was the pseudonym of Thomas Anstey Guthrie, an English
novelist and journalist.

9. Shere, Surrey, was a location the Allahakbarries played cricket in.

was a sight for Frederic to photograph, but he
forgot to pull the string or let down the lid or
something, and we all came out as a sunset in ye
olden time.

Partridge is the man who is to illustrate "New
Arabian Nights."[10] (By the by, almost the bitterest
memory of my childhood is the getting of the
other "Arabian Nights" under the belief that they
were Knights. Couldn't stand nights without a
K to them in those days, and indeed I have had
an ill-will to the book ever since). It is a capital
choice and he is full of the work. What a merry
jest illustrations to a book nearly always are. The
subjects the sagacious artist chooses! "He lifted
his hat politely." "She was sitting on a garden
chair drawing figures with her parasol on the
sand." "The butcher's boy had come to the door
for orders." "Allow me, he said." "In her walks
she was always accompanied by a mastiff of the
St. Bernard species." "She rose on his entry." "He
sat down on her departure."

Worse than the artists is my experience of
American publishers. Years ago I did cartloads

....

10. *New Arabian Nights* (1882) is a Stevenson short story collection,
which was divided into two volumes. Although the publisher Chatto
and Windus advertised a volume containing 'The Suicide Club' and
'The Rajah's Diamond' (from the first volume) in 1893, to be illustrated
by Partridge, the published volume in 1894 featured illustrations by
W. J. Hennessey.

of journalism at a guinea the yard, and they have
got at it, and publish a new book by me every
fortnight. Copyright they say and carefully
revised by the author. Rascally firm of Lovell,
another John Knox, who must have pirated even
his name.

Thomas Hardy

J. M. Barrie

Lady Colin Campbell

Mrs Clifford

Conan Doyle

This is not a tombstone, or rather it is.
Them five provided as many plays for a theatre,
all at one go, and were advertised as above.[11]
This was fatal, the public thinking we were the
company and refusing to go in because they had
never heard on none of us. Hardy dramatised
"The Three Strangers," and I had a bet that the
bill wouldn't run a week. It did—exactly.

Latest news as we go to press. Two magazines
want a Meredith at once and he is sitting up
in the chalet writing away against time, and as

11. From 3 to 9 June 1893, Terry's Theatre, London produced a 'Quintuple
Bill' of five one-act plays. Conan Doyle's *Foreign Policy* opened the bill,
and Barrie's *Becky Sharp* closed it.

flattered at anybody wanting him as if he had
arrived yesterday. Lang spells Alan Breck's
christian name with two ls and an e. Hurray!
I took Hardy to see my play at Toole's which
has been running about a year and a half and
warned him that a great deal of it wasn't mine,
and then had the mortification of seeing him
laugh heartily at the gags and at nothing else.[12]
Maarten Maartens was also with us, and they
both left the theatre saying that they thought
they could write successful plays.[13] Maartens
strikes me as one of the best men we have. Some
one has been telling Hardy you didn't like "Tess,"
and he sat reflecting a long time and then said
triumphantly "Methodist parson."[14] Extract
from a letter from Kipling about his infant
who was born on Gladstone's birthday, "As it's a
girl it doesn't matter, but if it had been a boy I
would have felt tempted to roll it up and down
in the ditch."[15] At least I'm told this is genuine.

....

12. Toole's Theatre was the name given to the re-opened Folly Theatre in
1882, named after J. L. Toole who acted in and directed some of Barrie's
earliest plays. *Ibsen's Ghost* and *Walker, London* were originally staged there.

13. Maarten Maartens was a Dutch writer who wrote in English; he was
a close friend of Barrie's.

14. Hardy writes of a 'Methodist parson' in his short story 'The Distracted
Preacher' (1879).

15. William Ewart Gladstone was the Liberal Prime Minister at this
point. The Liberal Party contained growing factions that critiqued

I'm sending you an illustrated "Window in Thrums."[16] The scenes are from life but the faces imaginary, also the blackbirds. I have found out where Samoa is on the map, which is a first step to coming. If I could only think of some place a great deal further away, that would bring Samoa nearer. The flower is to Teuila. Observe the colour. Goodbye Tamaitai, you have promised to like me. Goodbye, **Teuila, her mark.**[17] Goodbye Loia, though another has the photograph. Goodbye Tusi Tala. Goodbye my household.

Ever yours,
J. M. Barrie

---

imperialism, which did not sit well with Kipling's pro-imperialist stance.

16. An inscribed copy of A Window in Thrums is held in the Beinecke Rare Book & Manuscript Library, Yale University. The inscription is reproduced in the introduction of the present volume.

17. This sentence appears in red ink, mimicking the red ink Isobel Strong (Teuila) used in Letter 9.

11

[c. September 1893][1]

My dear Barrie,

My cousin, the bearer of this, Graham Balfour,[2] incessantly proceeding on his own affairs for England, takes to you, J. M. Barrie, seated in that inclement island, the greetings of,

Sir,
Your obedient Servant,
Robert Louis Stevenson

J. M. Barrie esq.
Kirriemuir, or wheresoever he may be found.

....

1. Booth and Mehew date this letter to roughly mid-September 1893 and believe it may have been written on the S. S. Mariposa [*The Letters of Robert Louis Stevenson*, VIII, p. 172]. On 12 September 1893, Stevenson left Vailima for Honolulu, Hawaii, where he spoke at the Hawaii Thistle Club.

2. Graham Balfour arrived in Samoa in midsummer 1892. He would go on to write the first biography of his cousin, *The Life of Robert Louis Stevenson* (1901), after Sidney Colvin—Stevenson's close friend— dropped the project following disputes with Fanny and Lloyd.

12

Vailima
Samoa

December 7th 1893

My dear Barrie,

I have received duly the *magnum opus* and it
really is a *magnum opus*.[1] It is a beautiful
specimen of Clark's printing, paper sufficient,
and the illustrations all my fancy painted.[2] But
the particular flower of the flock to whom I have
hopelessly lost my heart is Tibbie Birse. I must
have known Tibbie Birse when she was a servant's
mantua maker in Edinburgh and answered to
the name of Miss *Broddie*.[3] She used to come and
sew with my nurse, sitting with her leg crossed
in a masculine manner; and swinging her foot

1. A great work.

2. Barrie sent Stevenson Hodder and Stoughton's numbered edition of *A
Window in Thrums* (limited to 550 copies), which was printed by R. & R.
Clark, Edinburgh. The volume was illustrated by W. B. Hole, who also
illustrated several of Stevenson works, including *Catriona*. The item,
inscribed by Barrie, is held in the Beinecke Rare Book & Manuscript
Library, Yale University [Beinecke Library: item 7214].

3. A mantua maker is a dressmaker. A mantua was a loose gown in the
seventeenth and eighteenth centuries.

emphatically, she used to pour forth a perfectly unbroken stream of gossip. I didn't hear it, I was immersed in far more important business with a box of bricks, but the recollection of that thin perpetual shrill sound of a voice has echoed in my ears sinsyne. I am bound to say she was younger than Tibbie, but there is no mistaking that subtle indescribable and eminently Scottish expression.

I have been very much prevented of late, having carried out thoroughly to my own satisfaction two considerable illnesses, had a birthday, visited Honolulu, where politics are (if possible) a shade more exasperating than they are with us,[4] and generally employed myself upon what I suppose must be my Father's business for at least it's not mine. I am told that it was just when I was on the point of leaving that I received your superlative epistle about the cricket eleven. In that case it is impossible I should have answered it which is inconsistent with my own recollection of the fact. What *I* remember is that I sat down under your immediate inspiration and wrote an answer in every way worthy. If I didn't as it seems proved that I couldn't, it will

4. January 1893 witnessed the Overthrow of the Hawaiian Kingdom, a coup d'état whose insurgents were primarily foreign residents. This resulted in the establishment of the Republic of Hawaii, followed by the annexation of the islands to the United States in 1898.

never be done now. However I did the next best thing, I equipped my cousin Graham Balfour with a letter of introduction and from him, if you know how—for he is rather of the Scottish character—you may elicit all the information you can possibly wish to have as to us and ours. I believe you were also made a member of our great Temperance Society for the Consumption of Whiskey Punch,[5] and Balfour, who is perfectly qualified, will doubtless proceed to initiate you if he can find the chance and the punch. Do not be bluffed off by the somewhat stern and monumental first impression that he may make upon you. He is one of the best fellows in the world, and the same sort of fool that we are only better looking, with all the faults of Vailimans and some of his own—I say nothing about virtues.

I have lately been returning to my wallowing in the mire. When I was a child and indeed until I was nearly a man I consistently read Covenanting books. Now that I am a graybeard—or would be if I could raise the beard—I have returned and for weeks back have

....

5. It was while on the S. S. Mariposa between Samoa and Hawaii that the Mariposa Sanitary Association was proposed, advocating 'A Diffusion of Temperance Principles' and 'An Increased Recognition of the Claims of that Beverage known as Whiskey Punch'. The document appears in *The Letters of Robert Louis Stevenson*, VIII, pp. 169–71.

read little else but Wodrow, Walker, Shields etc.[6]
Of course this is with an idea of a novel; but in
the course of it I made a very curious discovery.
I have been accustomed to hear refined and
intelligent critics—those who know so much
better what we are than we do ourselves—those
who tell us it is time to stop working in l and to
work in b.c.[7]—trace down my literary descent
from all sorts of people, including Addison of
whom I could never read a word.[8] Well, laigh
i' your lug sir—the clue was found. My style is
from the Covenanting writers. Take a particular
case—the fondness for rhymes. I don't know
of any English prose writer who rhymes except
by accident and then a stone had better be tied
around his neck and himself cast into the sea.
But my Covenanting buckies rhyme all the
time—a beautiful example of the unconscious
rhyme above referred to.

....

6. Alexander Shields, Patrick Walker and Robert Wodrow were all
Covenanters or chroniclers of the Covenanters. I have retained Isobel
Strong's American spelling of 'grey' here.

7. Booth and Mehew note that this is a reference to the end of Barrie's
An Edinburgh Eleven, where Barrie instructs Stevenson to take life
more seriously in his writing and 'weave broadcloth [b.c.] instead of
lace [l.]' [*The Letters of Robert Louis Stevenson*, VIII, p. 205].

8. Joseph Addison (1672–1719) was an English poet, playwright and
politician.

Do you know, and have you really tasted, these delightful works? If not it should be remedied. There is enough of the Auld Licht in you to be ravished.

I suppose you know that success has so far attended my banners—my political banners I mean and not my literary. In conjunction with the three Great Powers I have succeeded in getting rid of My President and My Chief Justice.[9] They're gone home, the one to Germany, the other to Souwegia. I hear little echoes of footfalls of their departing footsteps through the medium of the newspapers. Here is a flower: "Is Robert Louis Stevenson in Apia you ask? The reply given with a shrug of the shoulders is that he has been away to Honolulu. He went to Honolulu for a change. He is writing, I understand, writing novels. He also writes a great deal about me. I don't know why it is—what purpose he has. It may be something personal against me. I do not know. I know he has written against me in short terms." O Barrie! What an overflowing sneaking love I have for a rogue! And how little humour there is in the world that I should be prevented

9. Baron Senfft von Pilsach (President of the Municipal Council) arrived in Samoa in May 1891; Conrad Cedercrantz was Chief Justice of the Supreme Court of Justice for Samoa from 1890.

from taking this lovely villain to my bosom now when trouble is over and the battle is won.

Whereupon I make you my salute with the firm remark that it is time to be done with trifling and give us a great book,[10] and my ladies fall into line with me and pay you a most respectful courtesy, and we all join in the cry of "Come to Vailima!"

My dear sir, your soul's health is in it. You will never do the great book, you will never cease to work in L. etc till you come to Vailima.

Robert Louis Stevenson

....

10. In *An Edinburgh Eleven*, Barrie claimed Stevenson was yet to write his 'great work.' With jest, Stevenson throws Barrie's criticism back at him.

13

Kirriemuir, N.B.

4 February 1894

Dear R.L.S,

Yours received this day at two of the clock.
Sat down to answer it at one (by the watch).

<u>Tamaitai</u>	Ah, Louis, if you could only—
<u>Teuila</u>	If he had such a cons—
<u>Tusi Tala</u>	I sit down to answer them at once also
<u>Tamaitai</u>	But you—
<u>T.T.</u>	Well, that is all he has done as yet himself, you know. And observe he brags about it, proving that it is not his usu—

I am not to be driven off my eggs by your
aspersions, and there are any number of them.
However, before I begin, listen to this. The
Ogilvy-Balfours a great family. Your mother a
Balfour, mine is an Ogilvy.[1] I needn't go into

1. Stevenson's mother, Margaret Isabella Stevenson (née Balfour),

details, but one thing clear is that Tamaitai is my cousin. Again, a reviewer has been comparing Catriona and Babbie to the disadvantage of my girl, but I forgive him as he gives me an idea, thus—

Very awkward, the idea can't go into the foot of a page.[2] I must fill up with padding.

An old Castle Balfour still stands in ruin three miles from Thrums. When Cardinal Beaton carried off a daughter of the Ogilvys from Airlie Castle, he kept her in Castle Balfour as his mistress *because* its towers are visible from Airlie.[3] Good, but not long enough. We had a heavy snowfall two days ago, but the rain has washed it away. Dang it all! The crops in the glens

---

settled in Vailima with Stevenson. Barrie would go on to write a book inspired by his mother, *Margaret Ogilvy* (1896), which included a chapter on Stevenson (see Appendix 5). She died within a year of Stevenson's passing, in September 1895.

2. Barrie wants to present his family tree on the Balfour-Ogilvy connection to Stevenson, but realises he doesn't have enough space to fit it in at the bottom of the manuscript page. He comically pads out this part of the letter and places the family tree at the top of the next page. The letter breaks off abruptly in mid-sentence.

3. Cardinal James Beaton (Archbishop of Glasgow and later St Andrews) and Marion Ogilvy of Airlie Castle (near Kirriemuir) fell in love in the 1520s.

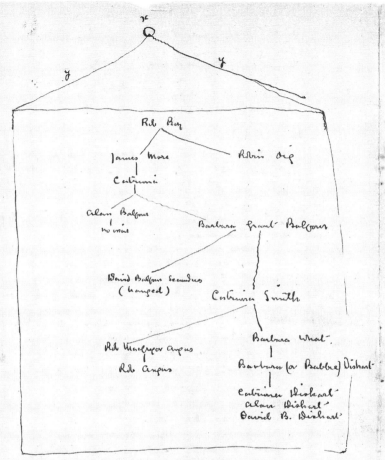

Rob Roy

James More — Robin Oig

Catriona

Alan Balfour / no issue

Barbara Grant Balfour

David Balfour Secundus (hanged)

Catriona Smith

Rob Macgregor Campus
Rob Campus

Barbara What

Barbara (or Babbie) Dishart

Catriona Dishart
Alan Dishart
David B. Dishart

The above to be enlarged on parchment
in red ink by Tenila and hung in the
hall at Verdure over the piano where Lou
sits for his photograph parcel concealed by Tenila
because he is not barefooted. It is a string
to hang it up by, and so is the nail. No
special finish is attempted in this sketch.
It is merely a suggestion.

Lou: But how can he know that when the photograph —
RLS: Unpunctual! Has my Brownie gone to Thrums!

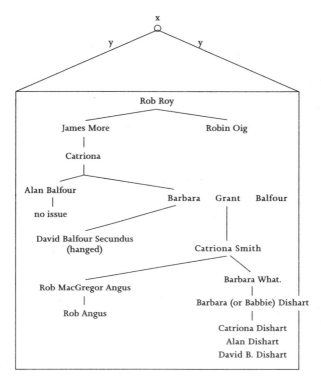

The above to be enlarged on parchment in red ink by Teuila and hung in the hall at Vailima over the piano where Loia sits for his photograph partly concealed by Teuila because he is not barefooted. Y is a string to hang it up by, and x is the nail. No special finish is attempted in this sketch. It is merely a suggestion.[4]

Loia   But how can he know that when that photograph—
R.L.S.   Dagont! Has my Brownie gone to Thrums![5]

....

4. This humorous family tree imagines Babbie Dishart, from Barrie's *The Little Minister*, as a descendent of Stevenson's character Catriona. Barrie imagines Rob Angus, a further character in *The Little Minister*, as descending from Catriona too.

5. A brownie is a household spirit that can turn malicious. Barrie mentions the Brownie of Badenoch in *Auld Licht Idylls*.

Opposite: Page 2 of Letter 13.
Edwin J. Beinecke Collection of Robert Louis Stevenson.
Beinecke Rare Book & Manuscript Library, Yale University.

I think there can be no question that the love story of Catriona and David is the best thing you have ever done. And it is just about the only thing I thought you could never do. All through the book I wanted to take Catriona aside and kiss her. (You needn't tell Tamaitai and Teuila this, but I never see a girl who strikes me as delicious without wanting to put my arms round her thoughtfully and kiss her. You can't always do it though. This is owing to the dissemination of pernicious literature). I consider David quite as good, far better than in "Kidnapped." Many like Barbara as much as Catriona, but no, she is only "Barbara, her friend," entertaining as possible, but I have met her often and though (see brackets above) still she usually had something to do with comic relief. I also liked her in the Black Arrow.[6] But Catriona is unique. I thirsted for more of Simon Fraser, and several others you are skimpy of, and that scene in the church at Inverary has made me chuckle more than anything since Vincent Crummles.[7] The Bass Rock story is creepy as you alone can make them.

6. Stevenson's *The Black Arrow: A Tale of the Two Roses* was an early novel, first serialised in 1883. Barrie may be referring to the character Alicia Risingham.

7. Crummles is the theatrical manager in Charles Dickens's *Nicholas Nickleby* (1839).

But James Stewart is behind a screen all the time, and neither you nor we care a doit whether he is saved. My earl and he should have been friends. "Dear Mr. Stewart, Can you take a chop with me at five, when we can discuss our grievances? Your truly, Rintoul. P.S. Both sawdust."[8] If Alan had been the prisoner, consider our excitement. Again, to me the beauty of the tale ends when James More opens the door of Catriona's and David's lodging. The atmosphere has been too lovely for us to endure him. I think the play of Rob Roy has spoilt me for Rob's sons. They are always one fair, one dark, one tall one short, one thin one thick, and how Helen MacGregor did send 'em flying. But you have one gorgeous bit near the end, when Alan kicks Monsieur. It is so exactly the right thing that never shall I forget the page and in what part of the page it is done. By the way, I always remember this latter if it is a great bit—in the Waverleys especially.[9]

Have at you again. (I have eaten and slumbered on the couch since the last paragraph.) While thus engaged a beautiful maid in the

8. Stevenson characterised Barrie's character Lord Rintoul in *The Little Minister* as superficial and unrealised in Letter 3.

9. The Waverley Novels are a series of texts written by Walter Scott between 1814 and 1831, the first being *Waverley* (1814).

bark of the mulberry tree,[10] and not too much
of it, appeared to me and said "O gentleman,
when thou comest among us, see to it that
thou breakfasteth in bed." And I said to her
"O lady where garments are wonderful but
most wonderful in this that they do not fall
off, wherefore?" And she said, "O gentleman,
because only such do we recognise as chiefs."
And I said to her, "O lady, if it were so Tusi Tala
would have warned me," to which she replied,
"O gentleman, not at all. He wisheth to be
considered the only chief himself."

Teuila   I know! Graham Balfour has been
            telling him things.

    Not so. I have not set eyes on the man, and
lately wrote him that I doubted whether there
really was any such person.[11] Yet we have been
on each others track for months, and there can
be no doubt we should have met by this time if
one of us had stood still. Twice he was to dine

10. Stevenson gifted ornamented mulberry bark to Barrie, which was
still hanging in his flat in the Adelphi, London when he died in 1937.

11. Barrie wrote to Balfour on 15 January 1894, noting that they
appeared to be playing 'a regular game of hide and seek'. In that letter,
Barrie describes Stevenson as the 'wizard of Samoa' and expressed his
hope that Balfour would visit him in Kirriemuir [National Library of
Scotland: Acc 12669].

PORTRAIT OF J. M. BARRIE
BY LESLIE BROOKE

Leslie Brooke's portrait of Barrie featured in The Studio *in 1897.*
Heidelberg University Library

143

with me, again I was in a studio being painted,
and he at the door, and the artist his cousin
(Leslie Brooke)[12] between us, and I talked to
Brooke about Balfour and Balfour talked to
Brooke about me, and we told him how we were
in pursuit of each other, and he never let on
because (O pitiful!) it would have ended the
sitting. Then just when I had him he went to
Edinburgh. I followed, and discovered he had
returned to London that morning or thereabout.
Have written him sharply that if he doesn't come
here pretty quick—But I shall have set off for
London. Just see if I haven't. He sent me some
of the mulberry bark, which now tapestrieth my
room, and your intimation that I was a member
of that Temperance Society which I divulged at a
Greenock Burns dinner. I enclose the newspaper
cutting there anent. Dang the thing, every time
I breathe it gets blown across the table, so I grip
it with the one hand and copy it with the other.
"Mr Barrie, in replying to the toast of his health,
said he wanted to put a question to the club.
(Cheers). Mr. Robert Louis Stevenson (loud
cheers) had lately sent him word of his election

12. Leonard Leslie Brooke painted a portrait of Barrie in this period
(which is now the property of Angus Alive). Barrie and Brooke met in
1892, and the portrait was reproduced in *The Studio* in 1897. Graham
Balfour married Rhoda Brooke in 1896.

to a Samoan Temperance Society established with two objects (1) to promote temperance principles (2) to encourage the exportation of Scotch whisky (loud laughter). What he (Mr Barrie) wanted the club to tell him was whether Mr Stevenson, without knowing it, had founded a Burns Club. (Prolonged applause)."[13] I'll send the cutting to Balfour. Even if it does get blown about, that may be the very way to find him.

Yes, you seem to have some pretty good villains at Samoa, and I cheer to hear you have got the better of some of them. That thundering hypocrite is quite fascinating, and I see you watching him go regretfully. But speaking of villains, also speaking of your one from the shoulder because I have been trifling so long. I am slogging away at a book at last,[14] and if I can keep up the last month's pace should see the end before so very long. But about villains. You are in it. I have long loved to picture you as a pirate of twelve or fourteen, and have now got my chance. You have a lieutenant who is also the crew (he is called Corp because he took fits)[15]

13. This speech was reported on in several newspapers, including *The Dundee Courier*, 27 January 1894, p. 5.

14. Barrie started devoting significant attention to his novel *Sentimental Tommy* in 1894.

15. Corp Shiach is a character in *Sentimental Tommy* (1896), three years

and two squares, and a puddle and a den full of fallen trees. You call yourself Captain Stroke because your lady teacher says "Stroke" when she comes across a word written thus "d—n."[16] Only so long as Tommy is a pirate is he you, but while thus I have precisely as I conceive you in those entrancing days. Not an ounce of humour left, the whole thing deadly earnest, and when Corp asks awestruck if you think it is all true, he is made to walk the plank. There is to be a great deal of childhood and boyhood, as I have never had a shot at that yet, but the general plan is a study of a sentimentalist who if he half conquers himself will do very well, I think. Am at a queer situation just now, a little girl going to several respectable gentlemen, and asking them not to come to her mother's house alone at night any more. You understand? There will be some painful matters in the book, but in no way will it be a surrender to the New Fiction, which so many are accepting as a short cut to greatness. Many of the new lady novelists might be divided into those who shriek because some one has seduced them and those who shriek because no

older than Tommy and leader of the 'less genteel boys of Monypenny' [Barrie, *Sentimental Tommy*, pp. 160–1].

16. In *Sentimental Tommy*, Tommy is instructed by Miss Ailie 'to say "stroke" in place of the "D—ns" [damn]' (p. 160).

one will seduce them. The novels it would seem, should be written with a part of the person not usually put to that use. Are you not beginning to feel strongly on that point? You would, if you were not away from the thick of it. And young novelists are being led into this guttery rut as the one worthy road (discovered at last) and I believe disastrous harm is done to women who think they are being told to think when they are really being told to brood. To brood about how it is done is so much worse than doing it.

I was just going to fire off another dream at you about a waterfall down which one scoots as if he were a toboggan, but I pull up at the sudden thought that you are in the scene all the time. Your mother writes you every mail, and if she has told you that I called on her in Edinburgh you will know where my information comes from.[17] Ah T.T.! if that was not Tamaitai saying, "We mustn't let on that we are laughing at him when he thinks he is mystifying us, it might hurt his feelings."

Stroke! No, str-k-!

17. According to Booth and Mehew, Barrie visited Stevenson's mother on 10 January 1894 [*The Letters of Robert Louis Stevenson*, VIII, p. 258n]. Margaret Stevenson set out to Scotland in January 1893 and started on her return in April 1894.

We are hoping to see your mother before long here. She and my mother want to talk about two boys, who had hooping cough, and did other extraordinary things. I think she is delightful. What do you think? Fain would I start with her in April, but my mother wants to go to London before I attempt Samoa so that she may judge for herself what these long journeys are like. My secret plan is in the autumn to go to America, get to San Francisco, and then sneak into a boat. That waterfall slide is irresistible altogether, and I want to get at it before there is an old lady sitting at the top selling tickets for it at sixpence each, which is no doubt what it will come to.

There was an amazing storm of wind in this and neighbouring counties two months ago, and I was not here to see.[18] It has blown down four-fifths of our woods. Our wood of 300 acres is entirely down. Gavin could look for Babbie for months in Caddam and not find her among those fallen trees.[19] The whole appearance of

18. In *Chronicles of Strathearn* (1896), Rev. John MacPherson notes that 'the great storm of 1893 has, indeed, laid low many of our finest plantations and marred the beauty of our scenery' [John Macpherson, 'At the Head of Strathearn', in *Chronicles of Strathearn* (Crieff: David Philips, 1896), pp. 157–82 (p. 161)].

19. Caddam Wood, which borders Kirriemuir, is one of the key settings in *The Little Minister*, and it also features at the end of *Sentimental Tommy*.

the county has been changed, gone back to
something more like what it was before Scotland
was planted. However, this gave me the idea for
your Pirate's Lair.[20] (You hang up a card inside
with that on it, and in your travels through the
den you observe the breadfruit tree which must
not be confounded with the deadly upas).[21]

I rejoice to hear you are planning a
Covenanting story. It is one of the few places
where Scott left an opening, for they could not
all have been whining hypocrites.[22] I would read
the fathers if I could get hold of them. But as for
your style I don't believe you got it from them or
any other book. You got it in our den when you
were playing at pirates. Playing! Unfortunate
word. Have you seen the new interviewing in
McClure's Magazine?[23] Two celebrities interview
each other and you have never heard of more
than one of them, but they play fair and the first
ass says, "And when Mr Some Man, did you feel

20. Stroke's Lair features in Chapter 24 of *Sentimental Tommy,* where a
'fallen tree' is mentioned (p. 276).

21. Upas are a tropical Asian tree, the sap of which is often used for
arrow poison.

22. Walter Scott set *Old Mortality* (1816) during the time of the
Covenanters.

23. *McClure's Magazine* was an American periodical that ran from
1893 to 1929. Stevenson's *The Ebb-Tide* appeared in *McClure's* in 1894,
followed by *St Ives* in 1896.

genius sprouting in your breast, and Some Man tells him when,[24] and then asks the second ass when *he* felt it and so on, with pictures down the sides showing "view of the coal-scuttle from the west window," "a corner of the press (with jug) flowerpot to the right on entering." But it is a nice little magazine for all that, and much better than our cheap ones.

Now goodbye. We have been talking in the *new* study, which I may tell you is in the new part of the house and was not built for you, but the light gets in more easily (no verandah covering). You have all got to come down the stair with me. This is the hall. (observe the piano). Mind the step. A last look round from the grass. Teuila is at the hammock. Tamaitai in the verandah. You are upstairs (old part). Waving a handkerchief (mulberry?) and off I go (barefooted) down the lane of citrons. But I see your red roof still.[25] Farewell, cousins, but I am coming back.

Ever yours,
J. M. Barrie

---

24. Barrie's handwriting is especially opaque here.

25. Stevenson's house at Vailima had a red roof.

Jean Franklin wrote that Stevenson posed as a pirate for this photograph [Beinecke Library GEN MSS 664 Series III, box 61, folder 1370]. In Letter 13, Barrie states that he based the persona of Captain Stroke in Sentimental Tommy *on Stevenson.*

Tapa cloth (made from mulberry bark), presented to Stevenson by Samoan natives. Stevenson gifted a similar example of decorated mulberry bark to Barrie, who had it hanging in his flat in London until his death in 1937.

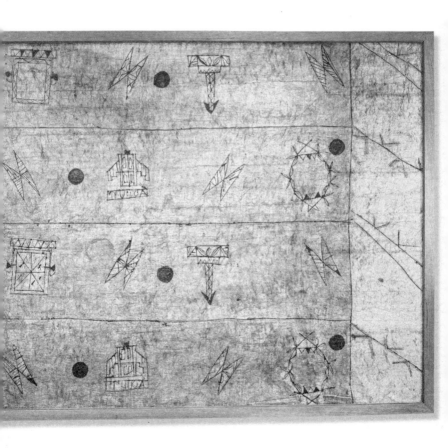

Edwin J. Beinecke Collection of Robert Louis Stevenson.
Beinecke Rare Book & Manuscript Library, Yale University.

14

[*Vailima*]

[c. March 1894]

Dear Barrie,

I will not say anything about your hand, because
my own is so damnable and apparently you
have no Teuila to temper the wind to your
correspondents. I will say nothing about your
hand I say, except that Henry James is easy,
and James Payn a gentleman alongside of you,
and the only person who writes worse is André
Bourget.[1] But not even friendship can prevail on
me to palliate the besotted ambiguity of your last.
It is like a beautiful letter I had the same mail
from some (plainly) very nice American boys,
out of which I could gather neither who wrote
it nor whence it was written. But even in that
case I could gather what it was about. Not from
yours. You *seem* in one paragraph to be clearly

1. James Payn was an English novelist and editor of *The Cornhill
Magazine*, which Stevenson published several essays in. Paul Bourget
was a French novelist to whom Stevenson dedicated *Across the Plains*
(1892). In 1886, Bourget published the novel *André Cornélis*.

meditating a descent on Samoa; and then in others, the beautiful seeming pales, vanishes with a melodious twang, and leaves us lamenting. The fault of obscurity is ... and on vital subjects too!

I duly heard from my mother of your visit. Did you see my Aunt? I recommend her to you for a study. Nothing could possibly please me more than a meeting between the two mothers. The Hooping Cough a grand subject; and will they no have their albums and press-notices to compare? A fountain of genial laughter arises at the thought.

> When the mithers of Alan and Ogilvy met
> The tea was untasted although it was set.

Your genealogy is no doubt quite exact. "Dishart" was a great *trouvaille*;[2] it is a noble name. I did very well with Hoseason, Shuan and Riach, in the brig *Covenant*.[3] Shuan was Free Kirk meenister of North Berwick, in his day, which was noisy, meddling and revivalistic. Riach was in the Auld Kirk—Riach of Pencaitland, the full

2. A lucky find.

3. Hoseason, Shuan and Riach are all characters in Stevenson's *Kidnapped*. They, and the protagonist, sail on the ship *Covenant*, which collides with Alan Breck Stewart's boat.

style of him, and I wished it could be supplied.[4]
I have another name in a projected tale, Blair of
Balmile; he was a genuine person, out of the '45.[5]
My own uncle has simply the finest name in the
world, *Ramsay Traquair*. Beat that you cannot. I
remember how much I adored Romeo the first
time I saw it, on sheets of characters (Skelts)
1 penny plain and 2d coloured.[6]

I shall keep secret your humiliating
confession as you request. "Put your arm round
her thoughtfully", the adverb is good. "You
can't always do it." No. You can't most always
generally do it, would be nearer the modesty of
nature. "This is owing to the dissemination of
pernicious literature." You bet! Shake hands.
I like Barbara the best, and so did David or very
nearly; but this was an infidelity—Hush!

....

4. Booth and Mehew note that Riach is a reference to William Lyon
Riach (1824–1912) and Shuan to John Shewan, Free Church minis-
ter at North Berwick from 1850 [*The Letters of Robert Louis Stevenson*,
VIII, p. 259].

5. Blair of Balmile is a character in Stevenson's unfinished novel, *The
Young Chevalier*.

6. Skelts' Juvenile Drama was a nineteenth-century series of scripts
featuring prints of key characters that could be used in toy theatre.
Stevenson devoted an essay to this series, 'A Penny Plain and Twopence
Coloured', which was first published in *The Magazine of Art* (1884) and
later in *Memories and Portraits* (1887).

All print my letters now—the Devil d— 'um!
Not for the Bookman, please, or Athenaeum.[7]

I am at
(1) The Justice Clerk (or else Weir of Hermiston).
About 50pp. done.
(2) The Young Chevalier. About 30pp.
(3) Heathercat (the Covenanting tale).
About 50pp.
(4) St Ives: Adventures of a French Prisoner
in England, on p. 93 and shortly to appear. It is a
mere story: to tickle gudgeons and make money
for a harmless fambly.[8]

The Justice-Clerk is, I fear, in rather the
guttery rut. At least the heroine disgraces herself
about as free as anyone I've heard of; and the
hero—but that's telling. Anyway, it's meant to
be best of them; that, or Heathercat. Would you
call it The Justice Clerk or Weir of Hermiston?
Perhaps the second is the best as the most
exact. But the other is the more Scottish and so
preferred by me.[9]

---

7. This couplet, warning Barrie not to publish the information that
follows, appears in the margins on the left-hand side of the manuscript.

8. A group of unrelated people who consider each other a family.

9. This letter is left unsigned, but it undoubtedly reached Barrie as he
responds to its contents in Letter 16.

15

Vailima

July 13th 1894

My dear Barrie,

This is the last effort of an ulcerated conscience. I have been so long owing you a letter. I have heard so much of you, fresh from the press, from my mother and Graham Balfour, that I have to write a letter no later than today or perish in my shame. But the deuce of it is, my dear fellow, that you write such a very good letter and I am ashamed to exhibit myself before my junior (which you are after all) in the light of the dreary idiot I feel. Understand that there will be nothing funny in the following pages. If I can manage to be rationally coherent, I shall be more than satisfied.

In the first place I have had the extreme satisfaction to be shown that photograph of your mother. It bears evident traces of the hand of an amateur. How is it that amateurs invariably take better photographs than professionals?

I must qualify invariably. My own negatives
have always represented a province of chaos and
old night in which you might dimly perceive
fleecy spots of twilight, representing nothing;
so that, if I am right in supposing the portrait of
your mother to be yours, I must salute you as my
superior. Is that your mother's breakfast? Or
is it only afternoon tea? If the first, do let me
recommend to Mrs. Barrie to add an egg to her
ordinary. Which, if you please, I will ask her to
eat to the honour of her son, and I am sure she
will live much longer for it, to enjoy his fresh
successes. I never in my life saw anything more
deliciously characteristic. I declare I can hear
her speak. I wonder my mother could resist the
temptation of your proposed visit to Kirriemuir,
which it was like your kindness to propose. By
the way, I was twice in Kirriemuir, I believe
in the year '77, when I was going on a visit to
Glenogil.[1] It was Kirriemuir, was it not? I have
a distinct recollection of an inn at the end—I
think the upper end—of an irregular open place
or square, in which I always see your characters
evolve. But indeed I did not pay much attention;

1. As Booth and Mehew note, '77 is most likely a mistake. From one
of his mother's diary entries, we know Stevenson visited Glenogil in
September 1871 [*The Letters of Robert Louis Stevenson*, VIII, p. 319].

being all bent upon my visit to a shooting-
box where I should fish a real trout-stream,
and I believe preserved. I did too, and it was a
charming stream, clear as crystal, without a trace
of peat—a strange thing in Scotland—and alive
with trout; the name of it I cannot remember,
it was something like the Queen's River and in
some hazy way connected with memories of
Mary Queen of Scots. It formed an epoch in
my life, being the end of all my trout fishing; I
had always been accustomed to pause and very
labouriously to kill every fish as I took it. But in
the Queen's River I took so good a basket that
I forgot these niceties; and when I sat down, in
a hard rain shower, under a bank to take my
sandwiches and sherry, lo and behold, there was
the basketful of trouts still kicking in their agony.
I had a very unpleasant conversation with my
conscience. All that afternoon I persevered in
fishing, brought home my basket in triumph,
and sometime that night "in the wee sma' hours
ayont the twal" I finally forswore the gentle craft
of fishing.[2] I daresay your local knowledge may
identify this historic river;[3] I wish it could go

2. A misquotation from Robert Burns's poem 'Death and Doctor
Hornbook'.

3. Barrie clarifies in Letter 16 that this is the Noran Water, which flows
through Glenogil.

farther and identify also that particular Free Kirk in which I sat and groaned on a Sunday. While my hand is in I must tell you a story. At that antique epoch you must not fall into the vulgar error that I was myself ancient. I was on the contrary very young, very green, and (what you will appreciate, Mr. Barrie) very shy. There came one day to lunch at the house two very formidable old ladies—or one very formidable and the other what you please—answering to the honoured and historic name of the Miss Carnegy Arbuthnotts of Balnamoon.[4] At table I was exceedingly funny and entertained the company with tales of geese and bubblyjocks. I was great in the expression of my terror for these bipeds and suddenly this horrid, severe and eminently matronly old lady put up a pair of gold eyeglasses, looked at me awhile in silence, and pronounced in a clangorous voice her verdict. "You give me very much the effect of a coward, Mr. Stevenson!" I had very nearly left two vices behind me at Glenogil: fishing and jesting at table. And of one thing you may be very sure, my lips were no more opened at that meal.

4. Balnamoon is situated seven miles east of Glenogil. The Carnegy-Arbuthnotts descend from two seventeenth-century Scottish noblemen and Privy Counsellors—Sir David Carnegy and Sir Robert Arbuthnott.

July 29th

No Barrie, 'tis in vain they try to alarm me with
their bulletins. No doubt, you're ill and unco ill,
I believe;[5] but I have been so often in the same
case that I know pleurisy and pneumonia are in
vain against Scotsmen who can write. (I once
could.) You cannot imagine probably how near
me this common calamity brings you. *Ce que
j'ai toussé dans ma vie!*[6] How often and how
long have I been on the rack at night and learned
to appreciate that noble passage in the Psalms
when somebody or other is said to be more set on
something than they "who dig for hid treasure—
yea, than those who long for the morning"[7]—
for all the world, as you have been racked and
you have longed. Keep your heart up, and you'll
do. Tell that to your mother, if you are still in
any danger or suffering. And by the way, if you
are at all like me—and I tell myself you are very
like me—be sure there is only one thing good for
you, and that is the sea in hot climates. Mount,
sir, into "a little frigot," of 5000 tons or so, and

5. Barrie developed both pleurisy and pneumonia in the spring of 1894
and his life 'hung by a thread' [Chaney, p. 118].

6. What I have coughed in my life.

7. Job 3:21 and Psalm 130:6.

steer peremptorily for the tropics; and what if the
ancient mariner, who guides your frigot, should
startle the silence of the ocean with the cry of
land ho!—say when the day is dawning—and
you should see the turquoise mountain tops of
Upolu coming hand over fist above the horizon?[8]
Mr. Barrie, sir,—'tis then there would be larks!
The fatted bottle should be immediately slain in
the halls of Vailima. And though I cannot be
certain that our climate would suit you (for it
does not suit some) I am sure as death the voyage
would do you good—would do you *Best*—and
if Samoa didn't do, you needn't stay beyond the
month, and I should have had another pleasure
in my life, which is a serious consideration for
me. I take this as the hand of the Lord preparing
your way to Vailima—in the desert, certainly—
in the desert of Cough and by the ghoul-haunted
woodland of Fever—but whither that way points
there can be no question—and there will be a
meeting of the twa Hoasting Scots Makers in
spite of fate, fortune and the Devil. *Absit omen.*

My dear Barrie, I am a little in the dark about
this new work of yours: what is to become of
me afterwards? You say carefully—methought

....

8. Upolu is the second-largest of the Samoan islands. Stevenson's
Vailima estate is situated to the north of the island.

anxiously—that I was no longer me when I grew up? I cannot bear this suspense: what is it? it's no forgery? And AM I HANGIT?[9] These are the elements of a very pretty law-suit which you had better come to Samoa to compromise. I am enjoying a great pleasure that I had long looked forward to, reading Orme's History of Indostan;[10] I had been looking out for it everywhere; but at last, in four volumes, large quarto, beautiful type and page, and with a delectable set of maps and plans, and all the names of the places wrongly spelled—it came to Samoa like Barrie. I tell you frankly you had better come soon. I am sair failed a'ready; and what I may be if you continue to dally, I dread to conceive. I may be speechless; already, or at least for a month or so, I'm little better than a teatoller—I beg pardon a teatotaller. It is not exactly physical, for I am in good health, working four or five hours a day in my plantation, and intending to ride a paperchase next Sunday— ay, man, that's a fact and I havenae had the hert

....

9. Barrie killed off the protagonist of *Sentimental Tommy* in the novel's sequel, *Tommy and Grizel* (1900). Barrie later noted in a letter to Cynthia Asquith that Stevenson's question inspired him to hang Tommy, who was partly based on Stevenson (as Letter 13 reveals). See *Letters of J. M. Barrie*, p. 190.

10. Richard Orme was an eighteenth-century historian of India. His *History of the Military Transactions of the British Nation in Indostan from 1745* was published between 1763 and 1778.

to break it to my mother yet—the obligation's
poleetical, for I am trying every means to live well
with my German neighbours—and, O! Barrie,
but it's no easy! I think they are going to annex;
and that's another reason to hurry up your visit,
for if the Herrs come I'll hae to leave. They are
such a stiff-backed and sour-natured people:
people with permanent hot coppers, scouring
to find offence, exulting to take it.[11] To be sure
there are many exceptions. And the whole of
the above must be regarded as private—strictly
private. Breathe it not in Kirriemuir, tell it not to
the daughters of Dundee! What a nice extract
this would make for the daily papers! And how
it would facilitate my position here! An idea:
suppose you printed it on the fly-leaf of your next
book?[12] It might conciliate or at least distract the
critics; me, it would distract with a vengeance;

11. Booth and Mehew note that 'hot coppers' refers to a parched throat
due to excessive drinking [*The Letters of Robert Louis Stevenson*, VIII,
p. 322]. Given the controversial content, it is unsurprising that these
two sentences were not included in Colvin's 1899 transcription of this
letter for *The Letters of Robert Louis Stevenson to his Family and Friends*.

12. This is a jibe at fellow Scottish author S. R. Crockett, who published
a fragment of one of Stevenson's letters in the fly-leaf of *The Raiders*
(1894), without Stevenson's permission. In the excerpt that was
published, Stevenson compared Crockett to Barrie, noting that 'The
Stickit Minister is out-of-doors, Barrie is within doors. By different
ways ye shall attain.' These Stevenson excerpts were also used as
promotional material in newspapers, including *The Scotsman*.

and it is quite in the practice of contemporary
Scots Letters. "The Professional Etiquette of
Scottish Authors; being a handbook of the
Courtesy and Chivalry practised by Scottish
Authors among themselves: with an Appendix
(315 pp) on the Art of Advertisment by—" ay,
by whom? He went up like a crocket and came
down like a stick.[13] Not but what I thought his
first book decidedly good, and was well pleased
with the dedication, and was fool enough to tell
him so in verses—which he is good enough to
publish for me,[14] and his publisher (at least) to
describe in a manner hardly to be reconciled with
fact. Well, well, *Tantae ne irae*?[15] (is that right?).

August 5th

To recover myself from these waters of bitterness,
this is Sunday, the Lord's Day. "The hour
of attack approaches." And it is a singular
consideration what I risk; I may yet be the subject
of a tract, and a good tract too—such as one

....

13. A pun on Crockett and his first volume, *The Stickit Minister* (1893).

14. In an 1894 edition of *The Stickit Minister*, Stevenson's poem 'To S. R. Crockett' was included at the beginning of the volume (apparently without Stevenson's permission again). The volume was dedicated to Stevenson.

15. Why such wrath?

which I remember reading with recreant awe
and rising hair in my youth, of a boy who was a
very good boy, and went to Sunday Schule, and
one day kipped from it, and went and actually
bathed, and was dashed over a waterfall, and he
was the only son of his mother, and she was a
widow. A dangerous trade, that, and one that
I have to practise. I'll put in a word when I get
home again, to tell you whether I'm killed or
not. "Accident in the (Paper) Hunting Field:
death of a notorious author. We deeply regret to
announce the death of the most unpopular man
in Samoa, who broke his neck at the descent of
Magagi,[16] from the misconduct of his little raving
lunatic of an old beast of a pony. It is proposed to
commemorate the incident by the erection of a
suitable pile. The design (by our local architect,
Mr Walker) is highly artificial, with a rich and
voluminous Crocket at each corner, a small but
impervious Barrie'er at the entrance, an arch on
top, an Archer of a pleasing but solid character at
the bottom; the colour will be genuine William-
Black; and Lang, lang may the ladies sit wi'
their fans into their hand!"[17] Well, well, they

16. Magiagi, as it is more commonly spelt, is a town in Samoa.

17. Stevenson references various Scottish writers here, beyond Barrie
and Crockett: William Archer, William Black and Andrew Lang. The

may sit as they sat afore, and little they'll reck, the ungrateful jauds! Muckle they cared about Tusitala when they had him! But now, ye can see the difference; now, leddies, ye can repent, when ower late, o' your former cauldness and what ye'll perhaps allow me to ca' your *tepeedity*! He was beautiful as the day, but he's by wi' it! And perhaps, as he was maybe gettin a wee thing fly-blawn, its nane too shune.

Monday August 6th

Well, sir, I have escaped the dangerous conjunction of the widow's eldest son and the Sabbath day. We had a most enjoyable time and Lloyd and I were 3 and 4 to arrive; I will not tell here what interval had elapsed between our arrival and the arrival of 1 and 2; the question, sir, is otiose and malign; it deserves, it shall have no answer. And now without further delay to the main purpose of this hasty note. We received and we have already in part distributed the gorgeous fahbrics of Kirriemuir. Whether from the splendour of the robes themselves, or from the

....

final clause is a reference to the Scottish ballad, Sir Patrick Spens, which includes the lines 'And lang, lang, may the maidens sit, / Wi' their fans into their hand'.

direct nature of the compliments with which you
had directed us to accompany the presentation,[18]
one young lady blushed as she received the proofs
of your munificence. Her position however was
delicate. Her father, an ambitious, loud, hearty,
dull man, comparable to a second-class Yorkshire
Squire, desired her to be united with Lloyd—and
still desires. Gifts of all kinds literally besiege our
portals; the last one was an (entire) Bull; some
say however, it is an ox; opinions halt. Strange
that there should be dubiety on a point so vital
and conspicuous! It is white, anyway; that you
may take on the authority of Tusitala; whether
or not it is really *faalavelave* (delicious Samoan
expression: lit, *hindered*) will require a closer
inspection.[19] In the course of these negotiations,
the young lady herself was sent to call; she found
it very embarrassing, and we found her very
pretty, and the (ahem!) towel was presented with
becoming words, and she blushed. Bad ink, and
the dregs of it at that,[20] but the heart in the right

18. One of the gifts exchanged between the two friends were fabrics from
Kirriemuir, a town known for its weaving industry. Unfortunately, the
whereabouts of Barrie's accompanying note are unknown.

19. Fa'alavelave are traditional extended family functions in Samoa,
often involving gift exchanges.

20. The writing on the manuscript is faint at this point, due to lack of ink.

place, still very cordially interested in my Barrie,
and wishing him well through his sickness, which
is of the body, and long defended from mine,
which is of the head and by the impolite might
be described as idiocy. The whole head is useless,
and the whole bottom painful: reason, the recent
Paper Chase.

> There was racing and chasing in Vailele
>   plantation
> And vastly we enjoyed it,
> But alas! for the state of my foundation,
> For it wholly has destroyed it.

Come, my mind is looking up. The above is
wholly impromptu.

On oath

Tusitala

> I le susuga
> a le alii Pali* (*Barrie)
> i lona maota i Tilimula* (*Kirriemuir)
> i Secotia
> Ua latalata ane i Lonetona[21]

21. According to Booth and Mehew, this translates as: 'To Mr Barrie, in

August 12th 1894

And here, Mr Barrie, is news with a vengeance.
Mother Hubbard's dog is well again—what did I
tell you? Pleurisy, pneumonia, and all that kind
of truck is quite unavailing against a Scotchman
who can write—and not only that but it
appears the perfidious dog is married.[22] This
incident, so far as I remember, is omitted from
the original epic—

> She went to the graveyard
> To see him get *him* buried,
> And when she came back
> The Deil had got married.

It now remains to inform you that I have
taken what we call here "German offence" at not
receiving cards, and that the only reparation I
will accept is that Mrs. Barrie shall incontinently,
upon the receipt of this, Take and Bring you to
Vailima in order to apologise and be pardoned for
this offence. The commentary of Tamaitai upon
the event was brief but pregnant: "Well, it's a

his estate at Kirriemuir, in Scotland, near London' [*The Letters of Robert
Louis Stevenson*, VIII, p. 324].

22. On 9 July 1894, Barrie married Mary Ansell in Kirriemuir.

comfort our guest-room is furnished for two."

This letter, about nothing, has already endured too long. I shall just present the family to Mrs. Barrie—Tamaitai, Tamaitai Matua, Teuila, Pelema,[23] Loia, and with an extra low bow, Yours

Tusitala

---

23. Tamaitai Matua was Stevenson's mother's Samoan name; Pelema (or Palema) was Graham Balfour's.

In Letter 15, after looking at a photograph of Barrie's mother, Stevenson asks
'Is that your mother's breakfast? Or is it only afternoon tea? If the first,
do let me recommend to Mrs Barrie to add an egg to her ordinary'.
The illustration above served as the frontispiece to
Barrie's book on his mother, *Margaret Ogilvy* (1896).

16

Kirriemuir

October 11, 1894

Dear R.L.S,

To tell you a great deal about my wife at once,
as soon as she saw your letter she jumped to the
last page because she knew that it would be the
page about her. That shows you she is a genius.
Furthermore she could not understand why I
laughed (she knows when I laugh) at Tamaitai's
prompt reflection about its being a comfort that
your guest room is furnished for two. Well, she
says, surely that would be the natural thing to
think of first. So you see she has a rich sense
of humour, indeed I never heard any one laugh
more heartily at her own jokes.

   We were rather crushed to find you in
possession of the news, having thought to
explode a bomb in the halls of Vailima with a
letter beginning "Fizz—izz—crack—boom—I
am married." I flatter myself that Loia exclaimed
fiercely "That chap!" and that Pelema became

limp and muttered "Dagont!" and that Tamaitai Matua made this memorable observation—

"What will his mother say!"

And then Tusi Tala and Loia (in collaboration) interviewed Pelema to discover whether he thought I was the kind to win a maid's affection and they found him in the Pa-wah-com luka (or morning room) all in a sweat because he was writing to Thrums (being his fifth go at the letter) and wondering, oh Gord, how to get to the fourth page without leaving a blank, and he said I was not the kind. Then they asked him if my conversation was of a kind to—and he said it was not of a kind to—and then they asked was ~~he~~ I insufferably handsome, and he had to admit with muffled curses that ~~he~~ I was.[1] And I expect myself that this was it.

I think your version of Mother Hubbard hits off my case pretty accurately. As for why we are not at Vailima at this moment I must refer you to Tamaitai Matua, who can guess. We really meant to make that our honeymoon,[2] but my

1. I have maintained Barrie's strikethroughs here, as they appear to be part of the joke, rather than mistakes.

2. Barrie and Ansell's plan to head to Samoa for their honeymoon was reported in the *Edinburgh Evening News*, 10 July 1894, p. 4.

mother was so doleful at the thought of my going
so far away that I had to give up the idea, and we
mooned about the Engadine instead.[3] There is no
spot on earth I want to go to much except the bit
of it that is yours, and to come I am determined
and as soon as I can get away. My wife is as keen
on it as myself, having set her heart on it as
soon as she heard you could go about barefooted.
You will find her an extraordinary storehouse
of inaccurate information. In character she
is so impulsive that she always begins in the
middle, and she is so remarkably like my
mother that that is probably why I fell in love
with her. Some faults she has. I notice that she
keeps her handkerchy and other articles in my
pocket, dropping them in and taking them out
without comment as if I were her dressing bag.
Her Scotch a little confused as yet: I heard her
asking my mother if a brae was a little stream
and whether there was any difference between
a garret and a burn. Nor is her handwriting
all that such a purist as myself could wish for.
I never find a letter addressed by her without
mending her letters on the sly, and this makes
her so mad that she uses language, including

3. Engadine, or Engadin, is a valley region in Switzerland where Arthur
Conan Doyle and his wife were staying.

the incomprehensible words, "You of all people."
She wanted to be amanuensis to this letter but I
told her you preferred it just like this.[4]

One day she—Is this letter to be all about
her? No. But when she read in your letter that
you had been down with the same ailment as
mine she remarked, "Don't let Mr. Crockett know
that, or he will take it too."

About that same Crockett it is related that
an old lady went into Mudie's and asked if they
could give her a book which was either "The
Crocket Minister" by Sticket or "The Sticket
Minister" by Crocket.[5] I was glad to read what
you had to say of him. I guessed that it was so
pretty much. This printing of private letters
is a shameful thing. But it was his first book
practically, and I suppose most of us are more or
less daft over our first. Do you know Crockett
personally? If you have met him once (or less
frequently) you are his bosom friend for ever,
whether you want to be or not. He sees to that.
I am his bosom friend. I can see it by his letters.[6]

4. Barrie responds ironically to Letter 14, where Stevenson characterises
Barrie's handwriting as the second-worst he has ever encountered.
Incidentally, Barrie's handwriting is much clearer in this letter.

5. Charles Edward Mudie founded Mudie's Lending Library in the 1840s.

6. Stevenson also received numerous letters from Crockett. The Beinecke
Rare Book & Manuscript Library, Yale University holds several.

Ever since I met him I have felt that he carries
me about in his pocket. I am writing this in one
of his tails to you in the other.

Ahem! As soon as I had read *The Raiders*
I knew it was not by Stevenson. Crockett is
downstairs. Stevenson is upstairs. By different
ways ye shall attain.[7]

Have you read an old book called *Peasant Life
in the North* by an anonymous McLennan?[8] If
not I want to send it you. I think it by far the
best book on the Scotch farm hand that was
ever written. Your mother told me, and I had
observed it with pain, that you never answer
questions unless one goes on repeating them,
so have you read a book called *Peasant Life in the
North*? I think it a great book.

To think of you having been here. It gives
me a new interest in the place. Possibly I saw
you. I may have flung a divot at you.[9] I have

....

7. Barrie jokingly invokes Stevenson's letter to Crockett (which was
published in the fly-leaf of T. Fisher Unwin's 1894 edition of *The Raiders*)
where Stevenson compared Crockett to Barrie: 'When I read the first
page of "The Stickit Minister"—the ploughing—I knew I was in Scotland, and I knew I was not with Gavin [Ogilvy]. The Stickit Minister
is out-of-doors, Barrie is within doors. By different ways ye shall attain'.

8. In 1891, Malcolm McLennan published *Muckle Jock and Other Stories of
Peasant Life in the North*, featuring stories he wrote in the 1860s and 1870s.

9. Barrie claimed to throw 'a clod of earth' at Lord Rosebery during
his student days, protesting his opposition to the Lords [Barrie, *An
Edinburgh Eleven*, p. 1].

been pointing out your abodes to my wife
(I knew she would come sneaking back into this
letter). On arriving at our station you cast your
eye across the line and noted the saw-mill where
my Rob Angus worked. I was almost certainly
there wading in the burn.[10] You then proceeded
up the beautifully named Marywellbrae (now
alas Mary Street because we are getting on so
well). You passed the foot of Chairlie Nicoll's
Roady near the house of T. Haggart humourist
who probably said a sarcastic thing about you.[11]
(Now I know why you say slighting things about
him). Your course then lay along Bank Street
where you passed the Auld Licht Kirk and if
you did not lift your hat to it, you are requested
to do it now. This took you to our square, at an
inn on north side of which you put up. That
was the Crown, landlord you remember a stout
man, name of Lennie. On your way to Glen
Ogil (now the property of one Williamson M.P.

---

10. In a speech on the opening of the sports pavilion in Kirriemuir,
which he gifted to the town, Barrie related the fact that he and
Stevenson may have been in the Kirriemuir together in their youth: 'He
was about eighteen at the time and I was seven. But oh, why wasn't I on
the outlook for him, if only to carry his bag to the station?' ['Barrie's
Present', *The Queenslander*, 11 September 1930, p. 64].

11. Unlike Haggart and Angus, Chairlie Nicoll doesn't feature in Barrie's
Thrums novels; he may have been a local figure or a friend of Barrie's
in Kirriemuir.

with whom I sometimes stay and henceforth shall stay with more interest, whose wife is a daughter of the famous Dr Guthrie)[12] you passed my Caddam Wood. The burn you fished was the Noran, famed for its clearness. There is no other water near. Possibly it is locally the Queen's River though I never heard it so called. I too have fished it. The Free Kirk where you were bored was the Kirk of Memus, and the man who bored you a queer character who died the other day, named Edgar.[13] In '77 was it? Then I had been here holiday making from my school at Dumfries. Heavens! I may have been fishing the Noran when you were there. There were three of us, all James's, but known as Jim, Jamie and Jeems and we searched the world for fish. If we saw you we probably bolted, thinking you were a keeper. You remember the woods at Glen Ogil? 100,000 trees were blown down there in the storm about this time last year. When you were at Glen Ogil did you happen to read a book

12. Stephen Williamson was Liberal MP for St Andrews (1880-85) and then for the Kilmarnock burghs (1886–95). Dr Thomas Guthrie was a Free Church of Scotland leader and philanthropist, who was born in Brechin, Angus in 1803. His daughter, Anne Guthrie, married Williamson.

13. Memus is a small town in Angus, north of Kirriemuir. Rev. Peter Edgar of Memus Free Church died in October 1893.

called *Peasant Life in the North*? I read it every
few months.

I think the *Ebb Tide* has extraordinary merit
as a narrative. Races along like a glacier stream,
indeed I don't remember any story that goes at
a greater gallop and that is a glorious thing in
a story, probably the greatest of all things. But
I thought the subject hardly worth while and
the characters too lurid, too much strongly
emphasised types. That is lovely where the
captain admits that his daughter has been dead
all the time. I vote for *The Justice Clerk* rather
than *Weir of Hermiston*, though it is good too.
Heathercat is fine, and makes me lick my lips.
I write it much more plainly than you do, and
so at last you have an opportunity of comparing
the titles just as they would look when printed.
I notice that by a slip of the pen you say my
writing is worse than James Payn's. Payn is
very ill and almost worn away, but still writing
funny paragraphs.[14] They carried him home
on a stretcher one night: He had fainted and
fallen and when the doctor came next morning
to see if he was alive he was sitting up in bed
turning the affair into comic copy. I think

14. Barrie submitted a story to Payn, 'The Body in the Black Box' (which
was rejected), when Payn was editor of *The Cornhill Magazine* in 1885.

him one of the sweetest of men. He told me
lately that somebody once dramatised his "By
Proxy." The final scene was the hero-villain
dying surrounded by the other characters. His
last words are "You thought me dead once before,
and by sacrificing another life I saved my own.
Now you see me dying again, but this time not By
Proxy." (Curtain)

I am wondering whether you have read a
book called *Peasant Life in the North*. It is the
strongest thing of the kind ever done.

Since my illness I have not done a stroke
of work till this week except a ghastly story of
Indian mutinies and stolen diamonds which I
raved about when I was delirious. I was in that
way for about five days, and I kept shooting
people and got into frightful passions because
those round my bed said they could not see the
corpses. All the time I knew that these corpses
were in a book which I was writing, and that
therefore there must be as many corpses as I liked.
I had a feeling of impotence because there were
no corpses when I, the author, had said that
there were. Did you ever have that sensation?
My mother is so very frail that I don't think she
could have lived had she seen me so ill. She had
bronchitis at the time and her mind was so

affected that she never knew it was I who was lying in the next room until I was getting better, when her mind was restored. I can't write about this without awe. It seems so much the kindly hand of providence. My mother is so frail that one must not even go near or touch her except with excessive gentleness. She has become so timid too. And she has an idea that where I am there she is perfectly safe. She is like a child in the matter. That is the only reason I have for not coming to Vailima just yet.

Our Correspondence Column

Tamaitai   It may be so. But that is not the only photograph I have seen, and one taken long ago that I saw at Miss Balfour's was quite lovely. I think it is a fearsomely strong face with a weakness somewhere—where I would walk in. This is presumption, but I have always felt that you are the one at Vailima who would like me best. I need such a lot of looking after and would be such a trouble that that face could not help liking me.

Pelema   (1) Your long and gossipy letter was a real treat.[15] I am not surprised that it took it

---

15. Barrie corresponded with Balfour from as early as 1894, and well into

out of you, but hope you are now restored to health. (2) I have not seen Brooke since his marriage. Am in hiding from him as he is still at the portrait.

Loia (1) I am sorry to learn that the native beauty has begun to cool, especially if it was my photograph that did it. Perhaps if you were to make-up like me? (2) I know of no safe ointment for producing hair on the face.

Teuila What has become of the red ink? I treasured your comments, which shed light on two people.

Native Beauty If you think it possible, try to forget me and love Loia again. But scorn to give him your hand if your heart is really in Thrums.

Tamaitai Matua Have no fear. My mother and she are tremendous friends.

Tusi Tala Yes, I can recommend it cordially. The title is *Peasant Life in the North*.

I never write to you nowadays without feeling that you are the only family in the world, outside my own relations, with whom I have a close tie. And I feel sorrowful when I end up, it

the twentieth century. Several letters are held at the National Library of Scotland [Acc 12669].

is always saying goodbye to you for a long time.
You must like my wife. You can't conceive what a
jewel she is. If Tamaitai only saw her putting in
my buttons! Would that she were taking them
out at this moment in the halls of Vailima.

Clgape wa-wa (farewell)
gug gug (dear ones)

J. M. *Barrie*

Appendices:
A Posthumous Friendship

'Scotland's Lament', by J. M. Barrie, 1895

*This poem was written by Barrie to mark
Stevenson's passing. The poem evokes the nation's
grief for its lost son, and it was published in
The Bookman within weeks of Stevenson's death.*

Scotland's Lament

Her hands about her brows are pressed,
She goes upon her knees to pray,
Her head is bowed upon her breast,
And oh, she's sairly failed the day!

Her breast is old, it will not rise,
Her tearless sobs in anguish choke,
God put His finger on her eyes,
And then it was her tears that spoke.

"I've ha'en o' brawer sons a flow,
My Walter mair renown could win,
And he that followed at the plough,
But Louis was my Benjamin!

"Ye sons wha do your little best,
Ye writing Scots, put by the pen,
He's deid, the ane abune the rest,
I winna look at write again!

"It's sune the leave their childhood drap,
I've ill to ken them, gaen sae grey,
But aye he climbed intil my lap,
Or pu'd my coats to mak me play.

"He egged me on wi' mirth and prank,
We hangit gowans on a string,
We made the doakens walk the plank,
We mairit snails withoot the ring.

"'I'm auld,' I pant, 'sic ploys to mak,
To games your mither shouldna stoup,'
'You're gey an' auld,' he cries me back,
'That's for I like to gar you loup!'

"O' thae bit ploys he made sic books,
A' mithers cam to watch us playing;
I feigned no to heed their looks,
But fine I kent what they was saying!

"At times I lent him for a game
To north and south and east and west,
But no for lang, he sune cam hame,
For here it was he played the best.

"And when he had to cross the sea,
He wouldna lat his een grow dim,
He bravely dree'd his weird for me,
I tried to do the same for him.

"Ahint his face his pain was sair,
Ahint hers grat his waefu' mither
We kent that we should meet nae mair,
The ane saw easy thro' the ither.

"For lang I've watched wi' trem'ling lip,
But Louis ne'er sin syne I've seen,
The greedy island keept its grip,
The cauldriff oceans rolled atween.

"He's deid, the ane abune the rest,
Oh, wae, the mither left alane!
He's deid, the ane I loo'ed the best,
Oh, mayna I hae back my nain!"

Her breast is old, it will not rise,
Her tearless sobs in anguish choke,
God put His finger on her eyes,
It was her tears alone that spoke.

Now out the lights went stime by stime,
The towns crept closer round the kirk,
Now all the firths were smoored in rime,
Lost winds went wailing thro' the mirk.

A star that shot across the night
Struck fire on Pala's mourning head,
And left for aye a steadfast light,
By which the mother guards her dead.

"The lad was mine!" Erect she stands,
No more by vain regrets oppress't,
Once more her eyes are clear; her hands
Are proudly crossed upon her breast.

APPENDIX 2
Letter from J. M. Barrie to Lloyd Osbourne, 1895

After Stevenson's death, his stepson, Lloyd Osbourne,
swiftly wrote to Barrie informing him of
the circumstances of Stevenson's passing.
This letter is Barrie's response.

Kirriemuir, N.B.

27 January 1895

My dear Osbourne,

It was with a very painful feeling that I opened
your letter the other morning, its outside with
the blue lines and many postmarks gave it such
a look of other letters I have had from Vailima
and such different ones. They all used to thrill
me when they came. "A letter from Stevenson!"
It stopped all work for the time and went the
round of the house. This is all done with now,
but I thank you very warmly for remembering
me on that mournful day. I have a sort of pride
in being among those you wrote to, for I take it
as meaning that to your thinking Louis would
have liked me to be one of them. As you may
know Colvin published your letter and he was

right to do so, for it told just what the public
were entitled to know. Your description of
the natives going and of the road making will
never be forgotten by any of us, and it had
a pathetic dignity about it, for it had Louis's
own mark on it.

The biggest tree in the countryside has fallen
some one said to me, and I suppose that is the
general feeling. Or if he was not the biggest tree,
for we have Meredith and Swinburne, certainly
the biggest tree in full leaf. And assuredly the
most loved and the one who has most influenced
his contemporaries. He was so gallant, such
a glorious boy that I think of him as a fifth to
d'Artagnan, Athos and the rest. Probably it was
for this that we loved him so much, though it
was for the qualities of his work that we sat at his
feet. To me it is as if a bit of myself had died, the
romantic part, which was for ever running after
him. The papers so far as they can do as [of] now
have seen what he was and said it ungrudgingly, I
think that his verse alone has not been esteemed
at its right value yet: I am not at all sure that it is
outshone even by the prose. I wish something
could be done for these Samoans. Obviously that
is what he would have liked of his countrymen
beyond all the honours, but it is so difficult to
make people here take their affairs seriously.

They are less real to Englishmen than Alan
Breck. They seem to look upon them as a sort of
picturesque background to Vailima. Balfour must
have seen this when he was here and no doubt
you have often discussed it. The news of Louis's
death came to me in a telegram to a Cornish
village where I have been staying, and was put
into my hands just as I had finished some verses
to him about his Edinburgh edition, lively verses
too. It was a pretty painful shock, and you know
how many of us would not believe it. I saw one
foolish letter in the papers on the subject, but
doubtless written in excitement that gave it a
form not intended. In his last letter to me he
said that he had finished "St Ives" but it was
short and not important. Of the Justice Clerk he
wrote full of hope, and I was glad you told what
he had said of it hurriedly on the last day.[1] I am
hoping that it is in an advanced state, and that
you know how it was to go. I suppose you will
finish it, and probably that would be wiser than
to publish it incomplete. But I write too much
from the outside to press this view. One thing

1. Osbourne related to Stevenson's friends that, on the day
he died, Stevenson was 'buoyant and happy' because he
believed 'his half-finished book "Hermiston" [...] the best
thing he had ever written' [Lloyd Osbourne, A Letter to Mr.
Stevenson's Friends (private publication, 1894), p. 1].

I feel strongly about is the biography that must come.[2] You who knew his life from day to day at Vailima almost as Boswell knew Johnson's, and there are so many letters, the autobiographical material is so rich, this diary he is said to have posted to Colvin should be so invaluable. It seems to me that a really big book of biography is again possible.

If we had come straight to you when we married we should have seen him, and because we did not I missed a great joy for ever. But though it has been a sad blow to me, I have not myself to blame, as I should never have hesitated about coming had not the health of my mother kept me here. And I always realised that something might happen. I should like to know whether you are all to make your home in Samoa still. I feel so sorry for your mother and his mother, it is pitiful that any of us should think of our loss beside theirs.

Yours ever,
J. M. Barrie

....
2. In 1899, Lloyd wrote to Colvin, listing Barrie alongside other potential candidates to write the life of Stevenson, after Colvin relinquished the task. Graham Balfour ultimately wrote the biography [A Stevenson Library, IV, p. 1527].

APPENDIX 3
J. M. Barrie's speech,
delivered at the Stevenson Memorial Meeting,
Edinburgh, 1896

*Barrie was one of several eminent speakers at
a meeting in Edinburgh on 10 December 1896,
which called for the erection of a national memorial
to Stevenson in the heart of Scotland's capital.
These efforts were eventually successful: the
Stevenson St Giles' Memorial (a bas-relief sculpture
by Augustus Saint-Gaudens) was unveiled by
Lord Rosebery in 1904. This report of Barrie's speech
appeared in* The Scotsman *the day after the meeting.*

MR J. M. BARRIE, who was received with loud
and continued cheering, said that he was so little
accustomed to public speaking that he had been
watching Lord Rosebery and Mr Lawson Tait
to try to find out what they did with their hands
when they were speaking. (Laughter.) He asked
them as a favour that they would allow him to
put his hands in his pockets to keep them at rest.
(Laughter.) (Mr Barrie there-upon put his hands
in his trousers pockets and kept them there while
he was speaking).

One of the inducements with which
Mr. Stevenson used to try to allure his friends
to Samoa was a waterfall, which the natives had
turned into a very remarkable and fearsome
plaything. They sat down on the top of it, and
were washed down with the torrent into a pool
beneath. The ladies went down as well as the
men, and Mr Stevenson used to say to his friends
when he asked them out that they must do so
also, just to show the fortitude of the Briton.
He always promised that a native lady would
go down with them the first time. Now if Lord
Rosebery had given him (Mr Barrie) a lead down
that waterfall, he was quite certain he should have
followed his Lordship with a lighter heart, and
certainly with less alarm than he felt in following
him that afternoon. Nothing would have induced
him to face this meeting; nothing would have
dragged him into the day-light had the cause been
less dear to him, and had he had less love and
admiration for Robert Louis Stevenson, who was
loved far more than any other writer of his time.
Those of them who were his adorers; those of
them who were Stevensonians, for it was a form
of freemasonry—those of them who made almost
an idol of this man, were very willing to admit
that he had imperfections, that he had failings,

that he was only mortal. But they had all read
in novels that a man when he was really in love
wanted the lady to know him as he really was, and
told her all that was to be told against himself—
what all his failings were; and he said to her
that now she could not love him so much. Then
he turned away from her in passion when she
admitted that she did not. (Laughter.) That was
how they regarded Louis Stevenson. They knew
that he had his imperfections, but if they believed
it they were all willing to turn themselves into
Alan Brecks and to become "braw fighters."

There was only one other novelist of modern
times who called forth such a passionate
devotion—a woman, a darker spirit than he,
one who died at a much younger age even than
he did, the author of "Wuthering Heights."
Everyone who had come under the spell of Emily
Brontë would fight on till the end.

It was no one single class that loved
Stevenson. All classes did. There was a beautiful
story of a little native boy at Samoa. When
Stevenson went there he built a small hut,
and afterwards went into a large house. The
first night he went into the large house, he
was feeling very tired and sorrowful that he
had not the forethought to ask his servant to

bring him coffee and cigarettes. Just as he was thinking that, the door opened and the native boy came in with a tray carrying cigarettes and coffee. And Mr Stevenson said to him, in the native language, "Great is your forethought;" and the boy corrected him, and said, "Great is the love." (Applause.)

That love which they had for him was just as conspicuous across the Atlantic. He (Mr Barrie) was in America lately—(applause)—and he found that they adored Robert Louis Stevenson there just as much as they did here. There was a window, as they knew, in San Francisco, where his works only used to be exhibited; and there were always great crowds round that window. He was told that there were women there as well as men, although Stevenson once wrote to him—"It is little the ladies fash about Tusitala and all his works. The ungrateful jades!" But that did not seem to have been so. Stevenson's chief appeal was to young men; it would be by young men he would be best known, and longest remembered.

It had been said that he cared little about his old University in Edinburgh. But that was not true. (Applause.) The other day he heard of a letter written by Stevenson to one of his oldest friends; it was written from the South Seas, and

he said he was lying in a boat, thinking of old days at Edinburgh University—(applause)—and the dreams he had dreamed in those days, and how little he thought at that time that they would be realised. And now that they had been realised, it had occurred to this friend that out of gratitude he might have put up at the corner of Lothian Street a tablet on which that little story might be inscribed, so that students who had grown down-hearted might perchance look upon it and be cheered. (Applause.) He (Mr Barrie) did not know whether that tablet would ever be put up, but he dared to say that many would seem to see it there and take courage.

He knew another body of younger men— younger men than Mr Stevenson, at all events— who took him as their model, who looked up to him as their example—he meant the young writers of to-day—(applause)—of all classes, not merely the Romanticists, but the Realists, as they were called; the Idealists, as they were called; the Pessimists, as they were called. They all agreed on one thing. They all saw with different eyes, but they were all proud of Stevenson, who, beyond all other writers, was the man who showed them how to put their houses in order before they began to write, in what spirit they should write,

with what aim, and with what necessity of toil. They knew from him that, however poor their books might be, they were not disgraced if they had done their best—(applause)—that however popular they might be, if they were not written with some of his aims, they were only cumberers of the ground. They were only soldiers in the ranks, but they were proud to claim him as their leader, and when he called his muster-roll they would be found answering to their names, "Here, here, here." Stevenson was dead, but he still carried their flag, and because of him the most unworthy among them were a little more worthy, and the meanest of them a little less mean. (Applause.)

Mr Barrie concluded by moving "That the following be requested to act as a general committee to promote the movement, with power to add their number:–The Earl of Rosebery (president); and further, that the following be invited to form an executive committee to carry these resolutions into effect, with power to add to their number:

Professor Masson (chairman);

J. M. Barrie, London;

Professor Baldwin Brown, Edinburgh;

R. Fitzroy Bell, Edinburgh;

Augustine Birrell, Q.C., M.P.;

W. B. Blaikie, Edinburgh;

Professor Bradley, Glasgow;

Professor Butcher, Edinburgh;

Edward Caird, Master of Balliol;

Sidney Colvin, British Museum;

W. Scott Dalgleish, LL.D., Edinburgh;

Principal Donaldson, St Andrews;

Professor Dowden, Dublin;

A. Conan Doyle, M.D.;

J. Dalrymple Duncan, Glasgow;

Richard Garnett, LL.D, British Museum;

Anthony Hope Hawkins, London;

Holmes Ivory, W.S., Edinburgh;

Henry James, London;

Professor Jebb, M.P., Cambridge;

Sir John Stirling Maxwell, Bart., M.P., Glasgow;

Professor Walter Raleigh, Liverpool;

Professor Smart, Glasgow;

Rev. Professor Story, D.D., Glasgow;

Lawson Tait, F.R.C.S.E., Birmingham;

Rev. W. W. Tullock, D.D., Glasgow;

Principal Ward, Owens College, Manchester;

Rev. John Watson, D.D., Liverpool;

J. H. Napier, solicitor, Edinburgh (secretary)."

APPENDIX 4
Letter from J. M. Barrie to
Margaret Isabella Balfour Stevenson, 1896

*Along with Barrie, Stevenson's mother was in
attendance at the Stevenson Memorial Meeting
in Edinburgh. After the meeting,
Barrie wrote this letter to her.*

20 Shandon Street
Merchiston
Edinburgh

10th December [1896]

Dear Mrs Stevenson,

That's over! And I hope I did not pain you.
I should and could have said so much more of
him. But it was a wonderful meeting and I was
thinking of you all the time as so many must
have been. And no one in Scotland has more
reason to be proud tonight as you.

Would Monday suit you for our coming
to lunch and was it 1-30 you said? We are so
looking forward to seeing you.

Yours truly
J. M. *Barrie*

APPENDIX 5
'R. L. S.',
from J. M. Barrie's *Margaret Ogilvy*, 1896

*'R. L. S.' is the seventh chapter from Barrie's
biography of his late mother. Since its publication,
the accuracy of Barrie's presentation of his
mother has been subject to debate. But what
is of relevance to this volume is the way Barrie
represents the irresistibility of Stevenson's writings.*

R. L. S. These familiar initials are, I suppose, the best beloved in recent literature, certainly they are the sweetest to me, but there was a time when my mother could not abide them. She said 'That Stevenson man' with a sneer, and it was never easy to her to sneer. At thought of him her face would become almost hard, which seems incredible, and she would knit her lips and fold her arms, and reply with a stiff 'oh' if you mentioned his aggravating name. In the novels we have a way of writing of our heroine, 'she drew herself up haughtily,' and when mine draw themselves up haughtily I see my mother thinking of Robert Louis Stevenson. He knew her opinion of him, and would write, 'My ears tingled yesterday; I sair doubt she has been miscalling me

again.' But the more she miscalled him the more
he delighted in her, and she was informed of this,
and at once said, 'The scoundrel!' If you would
know what was his unpardonable crime, it was
this: he wrote better books than mine.

I remember the day she found it out, which
was not, however, the day she admitted it. That
day, when I should have been at my work, she
came upon me in the kitchen, 'The Master of
Ballantrae' beside me, but I was not reading: my
head lay heavy on the table, and to her anxious
eyes, I doubt not, I was the picture of woe. 'Not
writing!' I echoed, no, I was not writing, I
saw no use in ever trying to write again. And
down, I suppose, went my head once more.
She misunderstood, and thought the blow had
fallen; I had awakened to the discovery, always
dreaded by her, that I had written myself dry;
I was no better than an empty ink-bottle. She
wrung her hands, but indignation came to her
with my explanation, which was that while R. L.
S. was at it we others were only 'prentices cutting
our fingers on his tools. 'I could never thole his
books,' said my mother immediately, and indeed
vindictively.

'You have not read any of them,' I reminded her.
'And never will,' said she with spirit.

And I have no doubt that she called him a
dark character that very day. For weeks too, if
not for months, she adhered to her determination
not to read him, though I, having come to my
senses and seen that there is a place for the
'prentice, was taking a pleasure, almost malicious,
in putting 'The Master of Ballantrae' in her way.
I would place it on her table so that it said good-
morning to her when she rose. She would frown,
and carrying it downstairs, as if she had it in the
tongs, replace it on its book-shelf. I would wrap
it up in the cover she had made for the latest
Carlyle: she would skin it contemptuously and
again bring it down. I would hide her spectacles
in it, and lay it on top of the clothes-basket and
prop it up invitingly open against her tea-pot.
And at last I got her, though I forget by which of
many contrivances. What I recall vividly is a key-
hole view, to which another member of the family
invited me. Then I saw my mother wrapped up
in 'The Master of Ballantrae' and muttering the
music to herself, nodding her head in approval,
and taking a stealthy glance at the foot of each
page before she began at the top. Nevertheless
she had an ear for the door, for when I bounced
in she had been too clever for me; there was no
book to be seen, only an apron on her lap and

she was gazing out at the window. Some such
conversation as this followed:–

'You have been sitting very quietly, mother.'

'I always sit quietly, I never do anything, I'm
just a finished stocking.'

'Have you been reading?'

'Do I ever read at this time of day?'

'What is that in your lap?'

'Just my apron.'

'Is that a book beneath the apron?'

'It might be a book.'

'Let me see.'

'Go away with you to your work.'

But I lifted the apron. 'Why, it's "The Master
of Ballantrae!"' I exclaimed, shocked.

'So it is!' said my mother, equally surprised.
But I looked sternly at her, and perhaps
she blushed.

'Well what do you think: not nearly equal to
mine?' said I with humour.

'Nothing like them,' she said determinedly.

'Not a bit,' said I, though whether with a smile
or a groan is immaterial; they would have meant
the same thing. Should I put the book back on its
shelf? I asked, and she replied that I could put it
wherever I liked for all she cared, so long as I took
it out of her sight (the implication was that it had

stolen on to her lap while she was looking out at the window). My behaviour may seem small, but I gave her a last chance, for I said that some people found it a book there was no putting down until they reached the last page.

'I'm no that kind,' replied my mother.

Nevertheless our old game with the haver of a thing, as she called it, was continued, with this difference, that it was now she who carried the book covertly upstairs, and I who replaced it on the shelf, and several times we caught each other in the act, but not a word said either of us; we were grown self-conscious. Much of the play no doubt I forget, but one incident I remember clearly. She had come down to sit beside me while I wrote, and sometimes, when I looked up, her eye was not on me, but on the shelf where 'The Master of Ballantrae' stood inviting her. Mr. Stevenson's books are not for the shelf, they are for the hand; even when you lay them down, let it be on the table for the next comer. Being the most sociable that man has penned in our time, they feel very lonely up there in a stately row. I think their eye is on you the moment you enter the room, and so you are drawn to look at them, and you take a volume down with the impulse that induces one to unchain the dog. And the

result is not dissimilar, for in another moment
you two are at play. Is there any other modern
writer who gets round you in this way? Well,
he had given my mother the look which in the
ball-room means, 'Ask me for this waltz,' and
she ettled to do it, but felt that her more dutiful
course was to sit out the dance with this other less
entertaining partner. I wrote on doggedly, but
could hear the whispering.

'Am I to be a wall-flower?' asked James Durie
reproachfully.[1] (It must have been leap-year.)

'Speak lower,' replied my mother, with an
uneasy look at me.

'Pooh!' said James contemptuously,
'that kail-runtle!'

'I winna have him miscalled,' said my mother,
frowning.

'I am done with him,' said James (wiping his
cane with his cambric handkerchief), and his
sword clattered deliciously (I cannot think this
was accidental), which made my mother sigh.
Like the man he was, he followed up his advantage
with a comparison that made me dip viciously.

'A prettier sound that,' said he, clanking his
sword again, 'than the clack-clack of your young
friend's shuttle.'

1. James Durie is one of the protagonists in Stevenson's *The Master of Ballantrae.*

'Whist!' cried my mother, who had seen me dip.

'Then give me your arm,' said James, lowering his voice.

'I dare not,' answered my mother. 'He's so touchy about you.'

'Come, come,' he pressed her, 'you are certain to do it sooner or later, so why not now?'

'Wait till he has gone for his walk,' said my mother; 'and, forbye that, I'm ower old to dance with you.'

'How old are you?' he inquired.

'You're gey an' pert!' cried my mother.

'Are you seventy?'

'Off and on,' she admitted.

'Pooh,' he said, 'a mere girl!'

She replied instantly, 'I'm no' to be catched with chaff'; but she smiled and rose as if he had stretched out his hand and got her by the finger tip.

After that they whispered so low (which they could do as they were now much nearer each other) that I could catch only one remark. It came from James, and seems to show the tenor of their whisperings, for his words were, 'Easily enough, if you slip me beneath your shawl.'

That is what she did, and furthermore she left the room guiltily, muttering something about

redding up the drawers. I suppose I smiled wanly
to myself, or conscience must have been nibbling
at my mother, for in less than five minutes
she was back, carrying her accomplice openly,
and she thrust him with positive viciousness
into the place where my Stevenson had lost a
tooth (as the writer whom he most resembled
would have said). And then like a good mother
she took up one of her son's books and read it
most determinedly. It had become a touching
incident to me, and I remember how we there
and then agreed upon a compromise: she was to
read the enticing thing just to convince herself
of its inferiority.

'The Master of Ballantrae' is not the best.
Conceive the glory, which was my mother's, of
knowing from a trustworthy source that there
are at least three better awaiting you on the
same shelf. She did not know Alan Breck yet,
and he was as anxious to step down as Mr. Bally
himself. John Silver was there, getting into his
leg, so that she should not have to wait a moment,
and roaring, 'I'll lay to that!' when she told me
consolingly that she could not thole pirate stories.
Not to know these gentlemen, what is it like? It
is like never having been in love. But they are
in the house! That is like knowing that you will

fall in love to-morrow morning. With one word, by drawing one mournful face, I could have got my mother to abjure the jam-shelf—nay, I might have managed it by merely saying that she had enjoyed 'The Master of Ballantrae.' For you must remember that she only read it to persuade herself (and me) of its unworthiness, and that the reason she wanted to read the others was to get further proof. All this she made plain to me, eyeing me a little anxiously the while, and of course I accepted the explanation. Alan is the biggest child of them all, and I doubt not that she thought so, but curiously enough her views of him are among the things I have forgotten. But how enamoured she was of 'Treasure Island,' and how faithful she tried to be to me all the time she was reading it! I had to put my hands over her eyes to let her know that I had entered the room, and even then she might try to read between my fingers, coming to herself presently, however, to say 'It's a haver of a book.'

'Those pirate stories are so uninteresting,' I would reply without fear, for she was too engrossed to see through me. 'Do you think you will finish this one?'

'I may as well go on with it since I have begun it,' my mother says, so slyly that my sister and

I shake our heads at each other to imply, 'Was there ever such a woman!'

'There are none of those one-legged scoundrels in my books,' I say.

'Better without them,' she replies promptly.

'I wonder, mother, what it is about the man that so infatuates the public?'

'He takes no hold of me,' she insists. 'I would a hantle rather read your books.'

I offer obligingly to bring one of them to her, and now she looks at me suspiciously. 'You surely believe I like yours best,' she says with instant anxiety, and I soothe her by assurances, and retire advising her to read on, just to see if she can find out how he misleads the public. 'Oh, I may take a look at it again by-and-by,' she says indifferently, but nevertheless the probability is that as the door shuts the book opens, as if by some mechanical contrivance. I remember how she read 'Treasure Island,' holding it close to the ribs of the fire (because she could not spare a moment to rise and light the gas), and how, when bed-time came, and we coaxed, remonstrated, scolded, she said quite fiercely, clinging to the book, 'I dinna lay my head on a pillow this night till I see how that laddie got out of the barrel.'

After this, I think, he was as bewitching as the

laddie in the barrel to her—Was he not always
a laddie in the barrel himself, climbing in for
apples while we all stood around, like gamins,
waiting for a bite? He was the spirit of boyhood
tugging at the skirts of this old world of ours
and compelling it to come back and play. And
I suppose my mother felt this, as so many have
felt it: like others she was a little scared at first to
find herself skipping again, with this masterful
child at the rope, but soon she gave him her hand
and set off with him for the meadow, not an
apology between the two of them for the author
left behind. But never to the end did she admit
(in words) that he had a way with him which was
beyond her son. 'Silk and sacking, that is what we
are,' she was informed, to which she would reply
obstinately, 'Well, then, I prefer sacking.'

'But if he had been your son?'

'But he is not.'

'You wish he were?'

'I dinna deny but what I could have found
room for him.'

And still at times she would smear him with
the name of black (to his delight when he learned
the reason). That was when some podgy red-
sealed blue-crossed letter arrived from Vailima,
inviting me to journey thither. (His directions

were, 'You take the boat at San Francisco, and
then my place is the second to the left.') Even
London seemed to her to carry me so far away
that I often took a week to the journey (the first
six days in getting her used to the idea), and these
letters terrified her. It was not the finger of Jim
Hawkins she now saw beckoning me across the
seas, it was John Silver, waving a crutch. Seldom,
I believe, did I read straight through one of these
Vailima letters; when in the middle I suddenly
remembered who was upstairs and what she was
probably doing, and I ran to her, three steps at
a jump, to find her, lips pursed, hands folded, a
picture of gloom.

'I have a letter from—'
'So I have heard.'
'Would you like to hear it?'
'No.'
'Can you not abide him?'
'I canna thole him.'
'Is he a black?'
'He is all that.'

Well, Vailima was the one spot on earth I had
any great craving to visit, but I think she always
knew I would never leave her. Sometime, she
said, she should like me to go, but not until she
was laid away. 'And how small I have grown this

last winter. Look at my wrists. It canna be long
now.' No, I never thought of going, was never
absent for a day from her without reluctance,
and never walked so quickly as when I was going
back. In the meantime that happened which put
an end for ever to my scheme of travel. I shall
never go up the Road of Loving Hearts now,
on 'a wonderful clear night of stars,' to meet the
man coming toward me on a horse. It is still a
wonderful clear night of stars, but the road is
empty. So I never saw the dear king of us all.
But before he had written books he was in my
part of the country with a fishing-wand in his
hand, and I like to think that I was the boy who
met him that day by Queen Margaret's burn,
where the rowans are, and busked a fly for him,
and stood watching, while his lithe figure rose and
fell as he cast and hinted back from the crystal
waters of Noran-side.

Appendix 6
Letter from J. M. Barrie
to Miss Rosaline Masson, 1922

*In 1922, Rosaline Masson published a collection
of reminiscences about Stevenson, titled* I Can
Remember Robert Louis Stevenson. *A short
piece by Barrie appeared in the first edition, where
he noted that he never met Stevenson and had no
right to be in the volume. After reading his own
entry following publication, Barrie decided to pen an
alternative entry, which he submitted to Masson with
this letter. Masson decided to publish the letter in the
second edition of* I Can Remember Robert Louis
Stevenson *in 1925. Barrie also related the story,
which parodies several Stevenson texts, at the Printers'
Pension Corporation dinner in 1924.*

Adelphi Terrace House

4th December 1922

Dear Miss Masson,

I am depressed to read my own fell admission
that I never saw or spoke to him. Such a galaxy
you have found, who even in the 'Seventies

(Scotch canniness) were qualifying for future admission to your pages, while I kept hitting my forehead in vain, to recall some occasion when I touched the velvet coat. Why did I not, for instance, hang about the Fleeming Jenkins's door? If only I had this much to go upon we should soon have got started.

Even without it? Why not?

It is a lasting regret to me that I met R. L. S. but once. This was in the winter of '79 when I was in Edinburgh, my first year at the University, Masson my great man. One snowy afternoon, cold to the marrow, I was hieing me to my Humanities, and was crossing Princes Street, nigh the Register House, my head sunk in my cravat, when suddenly I became aware, by striking against him, of another wayfarer. Glancing up I saw a velvet coat, a lean figure with long hair (going black) and stooping shoulders, the face young and rather pinched but extraordinarily mobile, the manner doggedly debonair. He apologised charmingly for what was probably my fault, but I regarded him with stern disapproval. My glowering look

was meant less for the chevalier himself
than for his coat and hair, which marked
him dandiacally as one of a class I had
read about as having dinner every day.
When he had passed he turned round to
survey me, and I was still standing there,
indicating in silence my disapproval of
his existence. He went on, stopped and
looked again. I had not moved. He then
returned and, addressing me with
exquisite reasonableness, said "After all,
God made me." To which I replied, "He
is getting careless." He raised his cane
(an elegant affair), and then there crossed
his face a smile more winning than I had
ever before seen on mortal. I capitulated
at that moment.

"Do I know you?" he enquired.

"No," I replied with a sigh, "but I wish
you did."

At that he laughed outright, and was
for moving on, when perhaps struck
by my dejection, he said, "I say, let us
pretend that I do." We gripped hands,
and then taking me by the arm (I had
never walked thus before) he led me
away from the Humanities to something

that he assured me was more humane, a howff called Rutherford's, where we sat and talked by the solid hour.[1] I had never been in this *auberge* (as he called it) before, nor have I been since, but I am sure it was a house of call of d'Artagnan and company in the days when they visited Newcastle and found it on the Scottish border. I associate that night indeed (for the afternoon wandered into night) with the four musketeers for various reasons, one being that we drank burgundy, and Chambertin at that, he reminding me that it was the favourite drink of Athos, and therefore the only drink for us, and when he ordered it he always said "a few more bottles" in the haughty Athos way. It was served in tankards and there was froth on the top, but we drank on the understanding that it was Chambertin. As for his talk, it was the most copious and exhilarating that I ever heard come from

....

1. Rutherford's was a public house on Drummond Street that was patronised by the Speculative Society, which Stevenson was a member of. Lord Guthrie notes that when society meetings adjourned, many members went out 'to buy pencils'—a euphemism for visiting Rutherford's [Lord Guthrie, *Robert Louis Stevenson: Some Personal Recollections* (Edinburgh: W. Green & Son, 1920), p. 33].

man's lips, and ranged over every variety of subject. You will be interested to learn that I was not one of those who let great talk pass on unheeded like a spate, to regret afterwards that I took no notes. I could write shorthand in those days, and I "took him down" in my class note-book (holding it beneath the table) till I had filled that bulky book. Alas that this record of wonderful hours should be lost. I lost it that night before we rose from the table. I had a vague recollection next morning that he had sold it to the waiter for a few more bottles of Chambertin. The waiter had proved to be a university student of my year, who valued, not the pages of the talk, but other pages about the Differential Calculus.

I say that the work was lost before we rose, but I have a notion that we rose more than once. The first time was the result of his discovery that someone in Edinburgh had said in public that he considered the works of Robert Burns to have an immoral tendency. Who this person was he had no idea; but my companion's proposal was that we should go out into the streets and

ring every door-bell until we found him.
The intention was then to argue with him.
We did go out (I think) and ring many
bells, but without success, and the snow
was still falling heavily, so I agreed with
alacrity when he proposed that we should
return to Rutherford's.

We had no more money (I had had
none from the start) but he sold them
his velvet coat for a few more bottles
of Chambertin. As the hours sped we
seem to have become quarrelsome, just
as Athos and his friends sometimes
did. I think the reason was that one
of us maintained that he was a "braw
singer" (I am not sure which one) and
insisted on putting it to the proof with
inharmonious results. I am certain that
I left Rutherford's pursued through the
blinding snow by my erstwhile friend,
who kept shouting "stop thief!" and
describing me (happily incorrectly) as a
man with a wooden leg and a face like a
ham. Long after all the rest of Edinburgh
was a-bed he was chasing me through
the white empty streets of the New Town
and the Old Town, and I was panting

hard when I at last reached my lodging in Frederick Street.

I had no idea of his name, nor would it have conveyed much to me, but I always longed to meet him again however risky it might have been, and I searched for him and for a velvet coat (for I suppose he had more than one). I remembered him as The man in the velvet coat until years afterwards, when I saw his portrait in a newspaper, and discovered that my friend of a night had been no other than Robert Louis Stevenson.

Alas.
Heigho.
It might have been.

Yours sincerely,
J. M. *Barrie*

Bibliography

BASE TEXTS

Letter 1: *The Letters of Robert Louis Stevenson*, ed. by Sidney Colvin, 5 vols (London: William Heinemann, 1924), IV, pp. 151–2

Letter 2: Manuscript—Beinecke Library GEN MSS 664 Series I, box 9, folder 234

Letter 3: Manuscript—Robert Louis Stevenson Museum, St Helena, California

Letter 4: Manuscript—Beinecke Library GEN MSS 664 Series I, box 9, folder 234

Letter 5: *The Letters of Robert Louis Stevenson*, ed. by Bradford A. Booth and Ernest Mehew, 8 vols (New Haven: Yale University Press, 1995), VII, pp. 412-4; supplemented by excerpts from the manuscript—New York Public Library Berg Coll MSS Stevenson

Letter 6: 'The Letters of Robert Louis Stevenson. Edited by Sidney Colvin. Life in Samoa:

November, 1890–December, 1894', *Scribner's Magazine*, 26.5 (1899): 570-87 (580-1)

Letter 7: Manuscript—Beinecke Library GEN MSS 664 Series I, box 9, folder 234

Letter 8: Manuscript—Beinecke Library GEN MSS 664 Series I, box 9, folder 234

Letter 9: Manuscript—Bancroft Library, UC Berkeley BANC MSS C-H 107

Letter 10: Manuscript—Beinecke Library GEN MSS 664 Series I, box 9, folder 234

Letter 11: Manuscript—Beinecke Library GEN MSS 664 Series I, box 1, folder 7

Letter 12: Manuscript—Beinecke Library GEN MSS 664 Series I, box 1, folder 7

Letter 13: Manuscript—Beinecke Library GEN MSS 664 Series I, box 9, folder 234

Letter 14: Manuscript—Beinecke Library GEN MSS 664 Series I, box 1, folder 7

Letter 15: Manuscript—Morgan Library and Museum, MA 4500; supplemented by 'The Letters of Robert Louis Stevenson. Edited by Sidney Colvin. Life in Samoa: November, 1890–December, 1894', *Scribner's Magazine*, 26.5 (1899): 570-87 (582-5)

Letter 16: Manuscript—Beinecke Library GEN MSS 664 Series I, box 9, folder 234

Appendices 2 and 4: Manuscript—Beinecke
   Library GEN MSS 664 Series I, box 9,
   folder 234

ARCHIVAL SOURCES

Beinecke Rare Book & Manuscript Library,
Yale University:
   GEN MSS 664 Series I, box 9, folder 234
   GEN MSS 664 Series I, box 12, folder 304
   GEN MSS 664 Series III, box 61, folder 1370
   GEN MSS 664 Series IV
   GEN MSS 1400 Series I, box 14, folder 488
   GEN MSS 1400 Series II, box 50, folder 1052
   GEN MSS 684 Series VII, box 29
   Stevenson 7214

National Library of Scotland:
   Acc 12669, Acc 13917/216

Centre for Research Collections,
University of Edinburgh:
   Coll 1549

PRINTED SOURCES

'All Sorts and Conditions', *The Dundee Courier*,
    27 January 1894, p. 5.

Asquith, Cynthia, *Portrait of Barrie* (London:
    James Barrie, 1954).

Balfour, Graham, *The Life of Robert Louis Stevenson*
    (New York: Charles Scribner's Sons, 1915).

'Barrie and Stevenson', *Muskegon Chronicle*,
    13 August 1894, p. 4.

'Barrie and Stevenson', *The Sunday Herald*
    (Boston), 12 August 1894, p. 27.

Barrie, J. M., *The Annotated Peter Pan:*
    The Centennial Edition, ed. by Maria Tatar
    (New York: W. W. Norton & Company, 2011).

— *Better Dead* (London: George Allen &
    Unwin, 1887).

— *An Edinburgh Eleven: Pencil Portraits from*
    College Life (London: Office of the "British
    Weekly", 1889).

— *The Little Minister* (London: Cassell and
    Company, c.1925).

— *Margaret Ogilvy* (London: Hodder and
    Stoughton, 1896).

— *Peter Pan and Other Plays*, ed. by Peter
    Hollindale (Oxford: Oxford University
    Press, 2008).

— 'Scotland's Lament', *The Bookman*, 1 (1895): 3–4 (supplement).
— *Sentimental Tommy* (London: Cassell and Company, 1924).
— *A Window in Thrums* (London: Hodder and Stoughton, 1924).
'Barrie's Present', *The Queenslander*, 11 September 1930, p. 64.
Burgess, Gelett, 'Mrs R. L. Stevenson Interviewed', *The Bookman*, August (1898): 122–4.
Catalogue of Valuable Books, Autograph Letters and Manuscripts etc., comprising The Property of the late Sir J. M. Barrie (London: Sotheby & Co., 1937).
Chaney, Lisa, *Hide-and-Seek with Angels: A Life of J. M. Barrie* (London: Hutchinson, 2005).
Colvin, Sidney, 'The Letters of Robert Louis Stevenson. Edited by Sidney Colvin. Life in Samoa: November, 1890–December, 1894', *Scribner's Magazine*, 26.5 (1899): 570-87.
Crockett, S. R., *The Raiders* (London: T. Fisher Unwin, 1894).
Dear Stevenson: Letters from Andrew Lang to Robert Louis Stevenson, with five letters from Stevenson to Lang, ed. by Marysa Demoor (Leuven: Uitgeverij Peeters, 1990).

Douglas-Fairhurst, Robert, 'Introduction', in *The Collected Peter Pan*, ed. by Robert Douglas-Fairhurst (Oxford: Oxford University Press, 2019), pp. xiii–xlvi.

Farrell, Joseph, *Robert Louis Stevenson in Samoa* (London: MacLehose, 2017).

Gifford, Douglas, 'Barrie's Farewells: The Final Story', in *Gateway to the Modern: Resituating J. M. Barrie*, ed. by Valentina Bold and Andrew Nash (Glasgow: Association for Scottish Literary Studies, 2014), pp. 68–87.

Guthrie, Lord, *Robert Louis Stevenson: Some Personal Recollections* (Edinburgh: W. Green & Son, 1920).

Hammerton, J. A., *Barrie: The Story of a Genius* (London: Sampson Low, Marston & Co., 1929).

— *J. M. Barrie and his Books* (London: Horace Marshall & Sons, 1900).

Hardy, Thomas, 'Robert Louis Stevenson', in *I Can Remember Robert Louis Stevenson*, ed. by Rosaline Masson (Edinburgh: W. & R. Chambers, 1925), pp. 214–16.

I Can Remember Robert Louis Stevenson, ed. by Rosaline Masson (Edinburgh: W. & R. Chambers, 1925).

Jack, R. D. S., *Myths and the Mythmaker:*

A Literary Account of J. M. Barrie's Formative Years (Amsterdam: Rodopi, 2010).

Jolly, Roslyn, 'Stevenson and the Pacific', in *The Edinburgh Companion to Robert Louis Stevenson*, ed. by Penny Fielding (Edinburgh: Edinburgh University Press, 2010), pp. 118–33.

Lang, Andrew, 'Recollections of Robert Louis Stevenson', *The North American Review*, 160 (1895): 185–94.

Letters of J. M. Barrie, ed. by Viola Meynell (London: Peter Davies, 1942).

The Letters of Robert Louis Stevenson, ed. by Bradford A. Booth and Ernest Mehew (New Haven: Yale University Press, 1995), 8 vols.

The Letters of Robert Louis Stevenson to his Family and Friends, ed. by Sidney Colvin (London: Methuen, 1899), 2 vols.

Lowson, Alexander, 'Echoes from the Sanctum', *Caledonia: A Monthly Magazine* (Aberdeen: W. Jolly & Sons, 1895), pp. 187–92.

Lucas, E. V., *The Colvins and Their Friends* (London: Methuen & Co., 1928).

Mackail, Denis, *The Story of J. M. B.* (London: Peter Davies, 1941).

Macpherson, John, 'At the Head of Strathearn', in *Chronicles of Strathearn* (Crieff: David Philips, 1896), pp. 157–82.

Maixner, Paul, 'Introduction', in *Robert Louis*

Stevenson: The Critical Heritage, ed. by Paul Maixner (London: Routledge & Kegan Paul, 1981), pp. 1–46.

McLynn, Frank, *Robert Louis Stevenson* (London: Hutchinson, 1993).

M'Connachie and J. M. B: Speeches by J. M. Barrie (London: Peter Davies, 1938).

Menikoff, Barry, *Robert Louis Stevenson and 'The Beach of Falesá': A Study in Victorian Publishing with the Original Text* (Edinburgh: Edinburgh University Press, 1984).

Meynell, Viola, 'Introduction', in *Letters of J. M. Barrie*, ed. by Viola Meynell (London: Peter Davies, 1942), pp. v–vii.

'Mr J. M. Barrie's Wedding', *Edinburgh Evening News*, 10 July 1894, p. 4.

Nash, Andrew, *'Better Dead*: J. M. Barrie's First Book and the Shilling Fiction Market', *Scottish Literary Review*, 7.1 (2015): 19–41.

Osbourne, Lloyd, *A Letter to Mr. Stevenson's Friends* (private publication, 1894).

Oulton, Carolyn, *Romantic Friendship in Victorian Literature* (London: Routledge, 2016).

Quiller-Couch, A. T., 'Mr Barrie's "Sentimental Tommy"', *The Contemporary Review*, 70 (1896): 652–62.

R. L. S. to J. M. Barrie: A Vailima Portrait, ed. by Bradford A. Booth (San Francisco: The Book Club of California, 1962).

Reid, Julia, *Robert Louis Stevenson, Science, and the Fin de Siècle* (Houndmills: Palgrave Macmillan, 2006).

'The Robert Louis Stevenson Memorial', *The Pall Mall Gazette*, 15 July 1898, p. 8.

'Robert Louis Stevenson Memorial', *The Scotsman*, 11 December 1896, p. 7.

Sanchez, Nellie Van de Grift, *The Life of Mrs. Robert Louis Stevenson* (New York: Charles Scribner's Sons, 1920).

A Stevenson Library: Catalogue of a Collection of Writings by and about Robert Louis Stevenson formed by Edwin J. Beinecke, ed. by George L. McKay (New Haven: Yale University Library, 1951–64), 6 vols.

'The Stevenson Memorial', *The Standard*, 14 July 1898, p. 2.

Tartt, Donna, 'On Barrie and Stevenson', *Fairy Tale Review*, 1 (2005): 66–71.

'Third Edition', *Freeman's Journal & Daily Commercial Advertiser*, 12 June 1897, p. 11.

Waller, Philip, *Writers, Readers and Reputations: Literary Life in Britain 1870–1918* (Oxford: Oxford University Press, 2006).

Acknowledgements

THIS BOOK BEGAN LIFE IN 2016 WHEN I
WAS A POSTDOCTORAL FELLOW AT THE
Beinecke Rare Book & Manuscript Library, Yale
University. I am deeply grateful to the Beinecke
for the fellowship opportunity and for the contin-
uing support and efficiency of the staff there. I am
also indebted to Christine Ferguson and Murray
Pittock for writing recommendation letters for
my application. Beyond the Beinecke, various
libraries and museums contributed to this project
through answering queries and providing access
to materials. I would like to extend my thanks to
the Bancroft Library, the Edinburgh University
Library, the Morgan Library & Museum, the
National Library of Scotland, the New York Public
Library, the Robert Louis Stevenson Museum, and
the University of Stirling Library.

This project wouldn't have been possible
without the support of the Estate of Robert
Louis Stevenson and the copyright holders of

J. M. Barrie's work. For their encouragement, permissions and input, I am deeply grateful. I would also like to thank the rights department at Yale University Press, as well as Ivon Asquith and Andrew Birkin, for their prompt responses to my enquiries. For their foundational work on Barrie's and Stevenson's letters, I am grateful to Sidney Colvin, Viola Meynell, Bradford A. Booth and Ernest Mehew.

At the beginning of the project, I wasn't sure if this short correspondence, comprising just sixteen letters, could ever become a volume. The encouragement of the following colleagues and family members made this book possible: Cathy Agnew, Jennie Batchelor, Kirstie Blair, Lucio de Capitani, Vybarr Cregan-Reid, Lesley Graham, Scott Hames, Sarah Hamlin, Hannah Knowles, Catriona Macdonald, Glenda Norquay, Cally Phillips, Mark J. Sanderson, my dad, Alistair Shaw, my sister, Lesley Shaw, and my grandparents, Alan and Isabel Stevenson. To Moira Forsyth and Bob Davidson at Sandstone, for instantly understanding the project and patiently sticking by it, I am very grateful.

Over the last few years, I frequently found myself wrestling with Barrie's handwriting and I often turned to family, friends and colleagues to

help decipher the more obscure words and phrases. I am grateful to many but particular thanks are due to Marco Biagi, Valentina Bold, Paul Geddes and Tom Hulme. For their dependable de-ciphering and proof-reading skills, I am especially indebted to David Taylor and my mum, Susan Shaw.

Scots Glossary

This glossary has been developed using the Concise Scots Dictionary, 2nd edition (Edinburgh University Press, 2017) and the Dictionar o the Scots Leid (www.dsl.ac.uk)

A' all
Abune above
Afore before
Ahint behind
Alane alone
Ane one
A'ready already
Atween between
Anent concerning/about
Auld old
Auld Reekie Edinburgh
Aye always
Ayont after
Besom/bizzom an ill-natured woman
Bit section/small amount/short while

Brae hillside/bank of a river/road
    with a steep gradient
Braw beautiful/fine/elegant/splendid
Brawer finer/worthier/handsomer/stronger
Bubblyjocks turkeys
Buckie shell/mollusc/something of little value
Burn stream/brook
By wi' it over and done/finished
Cam came
Canna cannot
Catched caught
Cauldness coldness
Cauldriff cold/causing or susceptible to cold
Chaff chatter
Cracks stories/chats/loud noises
Dagont confound it
Deid dead
Deil devil
Dinna do not
Divot a piece of turf/a peat
Doakens the dock plant
Drap drop
Dree'd endured
Een eyes
Egged urged
Elvint measuring rod
Ettled desired very much/was on
    the verge of/intended

Failed infirm/frail/broken down

Fash care/bother

Faur fare/favour

Firth estuary/wide inlet of the sea

Flow small quantity/few

Fly-blawn contaminated/dirty/unpleasant

Forbye besides/in addition to

Gaen going

Gar make

Garret turret/watch-tower/high place

Gettin getting

Gey large/excellent

Gowans daisies/wildflowers

Grat sobbed/wept/cried

Hae have

Ha'en had

Hame home

Hantle much/to a great extent

Havenae have not

Haver foolish/nonsense/to talk in a foolish way

Hangit hung

Heed pay attention to

Hert heart

Hieing directing

Hoasting coughing

Howff public house/favourite haunt/refuge

I' in

Ill trouble

Intil into/towards

Ither other

Jaud/Jade old horse/derogatory term for a woman

Joukit dodged/ducked

Kail-runtle a stem of kale, especially
    when hard and withered

Keept kept

Ken know

Kent knew

Kimmer girl/married woman/
    female friend/gossip

Kipped played truant

Kirk church

Lad/laddie boy/young man/son

Laigh low

Lang long

Lat let

Leddies ladies

Licht light

Loo'ed loved

Loup bend/jump

Lug ear

Mair more

Mak make

Makers authors/poets

Mayna may not

Meenister minister
Merried/mairit married
Mirk darkness/night/twilight
Mither mother
Muckle to a large extent/big/much
Nain own
Nane none
Ne'er never
No not
O' of
Ower too/overmuch/excessively
Pert bold/cheeky/presumptuous/daring
Ploys ventures
Poleetical political
Pu'd pulled
Put by set aside
Quo' quoth/said
Reck reckon/consider/heed
Redding clearing/tidying
Rime hoar-frost/mist
Roady road
Sae so
Sair sore/severe
Sic such
Schule school
Shirra sheriff
Shouldna should not

Shune/Sune soon
Shuttle mechanism in weaving,
    where threads are passed to and fro
Sinsyne since then
Sma' small
Smoored covered thickly/smothered/suffocated
Stickit unsatisfactory/disgraced/wooden
Stime glimmer or glimpse of light/
    faint trace of something
Stoup stoop/to bend over
Thae those
The day today
Thocht thought
Thole tolerate/endure/withstand
Thro' through
Trem'ling trembling
Twa two
Twal twelve/midnight
Unco very/strange/unknown
Wae woe
Waefu' woeful
Wee small
Weel well
Weird fate
Wha who
Whist shut up/to silence
Wi' with

Wid would
Winna will not
Wouldna would not
Ye you
Yestreen yesterday evening
Yon that

Dear Mr Stevenson